CRIB SHEETS

CRIB SHEETS

NOTES ON THE CONTEMPORARY ARCHITECTURAL CONVERSATION

EDITED BY SYLVIA LAVIN AND HELENE FURJÁN
WITH PENELOPE DEAN

THE MONACELLI PRESS
UCLA DEPARTMENT OF ARCHITECTURE AND URBAN DESIGN

CONTENTS

INTRODUCTION

A Con–
temporary
Cocktail

INTRODUCTION

just because you've read a new book on architecture recently doesn't mean it was contemporary, although many books have used the term or claimed its qualities. While there are plenty of new books on architecture, the discipline has no theory of contemporaneity, without which there can be no contemporary architecture. I'd like to promise you that *Crib Sheets* will provide one, but such a theory turns out to be a contradiction in terms. Even so, it's time for a provisional discussion of architecture and contemporaneity.

Architecture has had many different theories of time, most arguing that it has inherently bad timing. According to architects, architecture has never been on time: it is ahead of its time or working to stem the corrosions of time or monumentalizing the events of times long past or happily imagining a world without time or valiantly struggling to keep up with time or moving at a slow pace, slower than time, or embracing the supposed speed and spirit of the times. Some architecture has even been temporary, ephemeral, or just short on time. But to be contemporary—to be on time, to move with time and the times, subject to its losses, entropies, provisionalities, obsolescences, currencies, intensities, fads, and flourishes—is a possibility that architecture assiduously avoids.

What is strange about this evasion is that architecture has proven especially adept at identifying contemporaneity outside itself. From Le Corbusier and his cars to Venturi and his suburbs, from Eisenman and his Frenchmen, to Koolhaas and Condé Nast, architects have been avid chroniclers of the times of other disciplines and mediums. Their offices, desks, and publications are littered with pictures of fashions, shaped by techniques of industry, and are filled with sounds of music that are in their fullest flowering of time and at the apex of their desirability. Architects refuse to produce contemporary buildings, but they work hard to curate an atmosphere of contemporaneity.

Architecture is always on the prowl for contemporaneity, but never eats its prey. It likes to look mean but isn't dangerous. Architecture's talent for identifying the contemporary outside of the discipline ought to be harnessed into a new project for the field. Rather than merely pointing to the urinal of contemporaneity, like Duchamp, architecture actually needs to piss in the pot.

Contemporaneity is fleeting: by definition, it coheres for short periods of time and under particular circumstances. A theory of the contemporary is a theory of the flash in the pan. Architecture's self-image as arbiter of permanence thinly veils its fear of being a has-been, a fear that causes it to neglect the opportunities and intelligence of the flash. Flashes, like emergence, in today's parlance, require the coordination of innumerable factors. Not everything becomes a flash—most things remain stolidly in the pan. Flashes are not only short-lived, but they are jarring enough to overshadow their cause. Unlike the pan that appears self-evident, the flash appears mysterious, better described than theorized or explained, because it obscures its cause, not because it doesn't have one. In fact, flashes have more causes than other phenomena, coalescing infinite numbers and types of factors. While the pan is a simple and predictable response to conditions of perpetual concern, the flash quickly and efficiently calculates an enormously complex set of variables. Finally, the flash is simply more pleasurable than the pan: it is the performance rather than the stage, the special effects rather than the frame, perceivable but neither figure nor ground. Modernism likes pans because they are functional. Postmodernism likes pans because they are meaningful. The contemporary uses pots and pans but likes a flash

At the moment, a flashy pot to piss in sounds more alluring to me than any other theory of architecture. A new mode of speculation needs to be whipped up that seeks not to stabilize, historicize, or philosophize concepts but to activate them. The first step in giving architecture a theory of contemporaneity is recognizing that traditional forms of theory are even more resistant to contemporaneity than architecture. Their goal has always been to produce concepts, measuring their value in terms of longevity. So a theory of contemporaneity cannot be another, or merely new, theory but must begin by making theory itself contemporary. In fact, a theory of contemporaneity will turn theory into criticism, which ought not to be understood as applied theory, but as the only discursive technique in sync with architecture today. Venturi learned from Las Vegas, but by the end of the lesson the strip had become a new road to old Rome. Today, if you're looking for flash, you can look everywhere. You don't need to go to Vegas and you don't need to go to Rome. You don't need to leave your living room couch: just turn up MTV *Cribs* and listen to B2K say that wood trim can make any home seem like a museum. Then you have caught flash: an extraordinarily seamless amalgam of realism, fantasy, design, voyeurism, technology, display, slumming, up-styling, and architecture.

Trading in the sobriety of academic rhetoric for a cocktail-party mood is the first tactic in the shift from theory to criticism. We've had some good parties at UCLA's Department of Architecture and Urban Design over the past ten years. But no mere analogy, the cocktail party offers to discourse a contemporary diagram. Coalescing social milieus, current events, nodes, and clusters of topics, avoiding method and classification, using background noise, eavesdropping, and affective language, the cocktail party produces unadulterated arguments. But cocktail parties are for adults only: they are knowing rather than knowledgeable. No one offers footnotes at a cocktail party, or brings proof or acknowledges sources. Cocktail party discourse does not observe distinctions between evidence and speculation but rather harnesses extreme rhetorical form to make even the most baseless rumor seem plausible. And in that promiscuous productivity lies its promise.

One of UCLA's best parties was a conference called "The Good, the Bad, and the Beautiful." Faculty, outside critics, and students were invited. In the transcripts, certain terms came to the fore not because they provided the best evidence of contested terrains or an exhaustive survey of theoretical terms, but because they buzzed with the mood of the event. *Crib Sheets* presents twenty-two of our favorites and brings these buzzwords together with introductions and comments by the UCLA crowd, which includes not only students and faculty, but friends and colleagues we've hosted over the years, acquaintances, and authors we like to read. The setting is provided by a slightly inebriated collection of contemporary images. Other institutions over recent years have served up similar cocktails, but *Crib Sheets* is UCLA's particular concoction.

Like all buzzwords, those in *Crib Sheets* will be denigrated for being superficial, unlearned, evasive, and reductive. But their superficial, unlearned, evasive, and reductive flash intensifies, distills, coordinates, and disseminates an unthinkably wide array of meanings and other affects. It's a fact of life that buzzwords are the most efficient instrument for setting into motion the mood of an idea. Go back and look at your Cliff Notes: they aren't bad. And whether you use them to study or cheat, producing good crib sheets takes talent. Within the contemporary, crib sheets take the place of theory, abbreviating its histories, concepts, processes, and truths into buzzwords, conjectures, and productions, measuring its achievements in terms of failures and flashes. In short, like architecture, a crib sheet is designed. And in time, we hope that *Crib Sheets* will turn out to be like architecture, born and dead like a flash in the pan.

TERMS

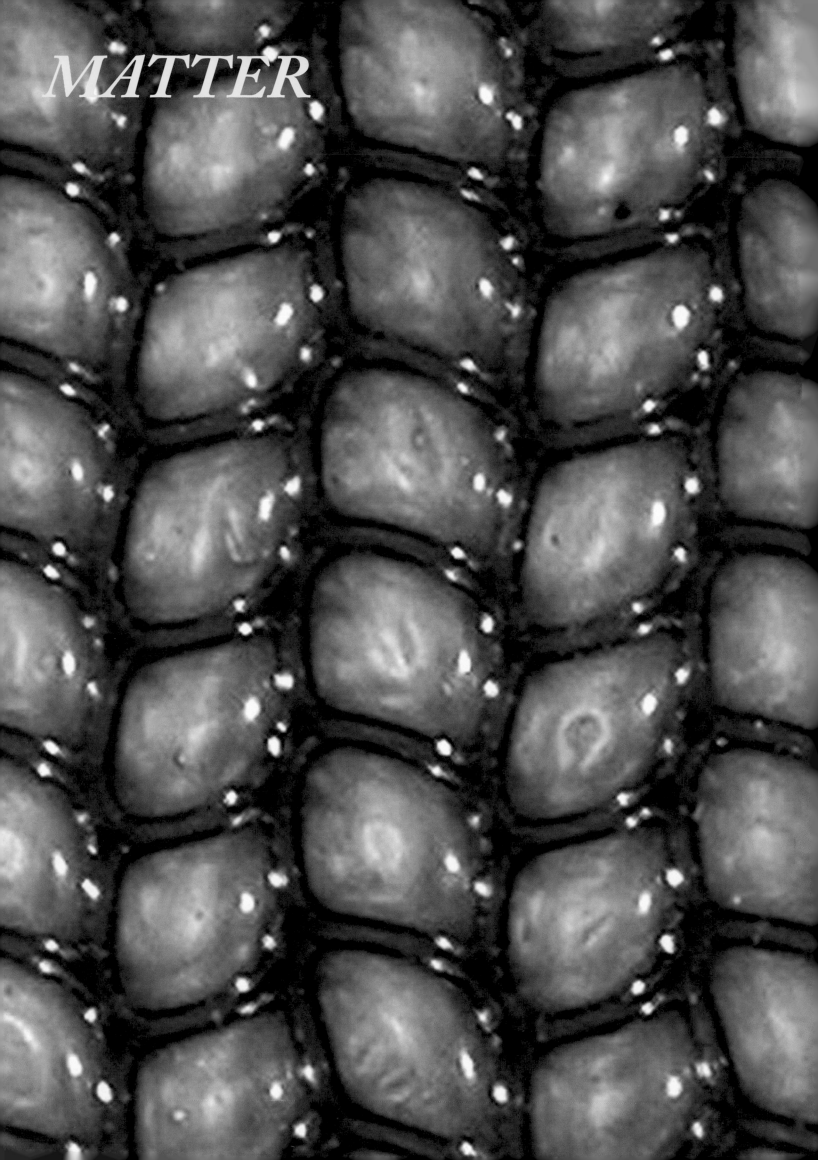
MATTER

Genuine plastic

Matter, one could say, is the new space.

MATTER

2. Sheila Kennedy
Robust and ethereal; substantial and dissolving; part insect gossamer, part human flesh, part profoundly other . . .

3. Ellen Lupton
Injections of fat or collagen are used to temporarily fill shallow lines and acne scars.

4. Gilles Deleuze
In the unity of the catastrophe and the diagram, man discovers rhythm as matter and material.

5. Clover Lee
Material : Matter
Scale : Scale-less
Dimensional : Phenomenal
Depictive : Ambiguous
Assembly : Part-less
Substantive: Disembodied
Static : Volatile
Definitive : Ambiguous
Prototypical : Anomalous

6. William Gibson
Rain-silvered plywood, broken marble from the walls of forgotten banks, corrugated plastic, polished brass, sequins, painted canvas, mirrors, chrome gone dull and peeling in the salt air.

7. Jesse Reiser
Instead of viewing the building in terms of representation or symbolisation, what is at stake is its own internal economy. Change thus becomes an active expression of the material organisation of the building.

8. Heather Roberge
The development of matter rich enough to produce side effects of architectural value tends to amplify the qualitative, substantive aspects of material organizations. At the same time, conceptual and representational issues tend to be forced out: substance in, concept out.

9. Hugh Ferriss
BUILDINGS like crystals.
Walls of translucent glass.
Sheer glass blocks sheathing a steel grill.
No Gothic branch: no Acanthus leaf: no recollection of the plant world.
No mineral kingdom.
Gleaming stalagmites.
Forms as cold as ice.
Mathematics.
Night in the Science Zone.

10. Mark Goulthorpe
Increasingly, I think of a project as a distribution of material in space, not as the assemblage of preformed elements. We're moving from collage to morphology, looking to deploy material as material for its spatial and surface effects and culling the potential of crystallization or sublimation.

11. Manuel De Landa
Deleuze's philosophy of matter and form, a philosophy which attempts to replace essentialist views of the genesis of form (which imply a conception of matter as an inert receptacle for forms that come from the outside) with one in which matter is already pregnant with morphogenetic capabilities, therefore capable of generating form on its own.

12. Jeffrey Kipnis
In the simplest terms, the radicalization of matter requires three recognitions: that matter is from the beginning irreducibly sensate and responsive; that at every scale sensate, responsive matter organizes itself hierarchically into discreet, irreproducible configurations with specific emergent behaviors; and that all discreet material configurations at any and every moment and any and every scale further arrange into complex ecologies.

13. Gilles Deleuze and Félix Guattari

An abstract machine in itself is not physical or corporeal, any more than it is semiotic; it is *diagrammatic* (it knows nothing of the distinction between the artificial and the natural either). It operates by *matter*, not by substance; by *function*, not by form. The abstract machine is pure Matter-Function—a diagram independent of the forms and substances, expressions and contents it will distribute.

14. Craig Hodgetts

In recent years, from the standpoint of material utilization, buildings have begun doing a lot more with a lot less. Pound-for-pound, hour-by-hour, and inch-by-inch, there is simply no comparison between today's buildings and those of a quarter-century ago. That said, its most unfortunate that the purposes for which we build have not yet caught up with the transmutational impact of the Internet and the PC.

15. Alejandro Zaera-Polo

Architecture is not a plastic art, but the engineering of material life. In our practice, our main concern is to produce consistency in the process of construction and material organization rather than in its plastic effects. In fact, we are not interested in producing preconceived effects, but rather in exploring materials—and here material should be understood in the broadest possible sense—as a source of ideas and effects.

16. Bruce Sterling

Virtual reality offers unique design opportunities, because virtual reality has no material constraints. There's no material in it, by definition. It's all just moving pixels, so something can look like anything; all it takes is someone willing to invest the time and effort to make it look that way. Nothing ever rusts, nothing breaks, nothing collapses; it just gets diskwiped. There are no laws of physics in virtual reality, no entropy, no friction. Virtual environments, therefore, can absorb infinite amounts of manpower, infinite amounts of design ingenuity.

17. Jesse Reiser

Conceiving matter in all of its changes, transformations and richness is a very different mode of thinking architectural organization than Idealism, which even when it locks on to certain structures, reducing them to constants and invariants—in other words, to ideas. We are interested in a new conception of universality, not based upon the ideal as universal, but rather upon the materialist notion of the space of ubiquitous difference. This involves a transition from imagining space as an abstract thing, which is framed, to imagining space as matter itself.

18. Johan Bettum

The possibility of addressing matter as opposed to materials in architectural discourse signifies a radical shift of scale from the macro realm of meters to the micro realm of fractions of a millimeter. This shift is the result of developments in both material and industrial processing technology and heralds new frontiers for architects to grapple with. "Matter" also expresses a long-awaited manifestation of radical sensibility in architecture, an emergence whose advent can be dated to a pre-Modern era when the politics of the body emerged in European discourse (in the writing of Georges Bataille, for instance). A preoccupation with matter is long overdue.

19. Michael Bell

If there is one realm of architecture left underexamined; it is matter. The meticulous detailing of projects via cad models seems to be accomplished in the professional strata that leads from schematic design to construction drawings: in other words, matter arrives as a supplement to design and at the end of design. It is easy to find matter in Louis Kahn or Rafael Moneo—and it is perhaps easy to also reject a model of physics that would permeate matter early in a project as a mode of local gravity or weight. But a significant strain of a contemporary bibliography in architectural theory is based in theories of matter: Henri Focillon, Henri Bergson, Deleuze on Bergson, Whitehead, Hejduk's invocations of density and opacity, or Rosalind Krauss's readings of entropy in Robert Smithson, Michael Heizer and Robert Morris . . . Matter, as a form of perception and time, alters how early material, weight, and shape enter a design process.

MATTER

20. Jason Payne

Manuel DeLanda has suggested that built form exists as the highest level of geological articulation of the earth's crust. Assuming this to be the case, the continually shifting methodological terrains of architectural practice are enmeshed within the much slower but no less inexorable flows of soil, rocks, water, biomass, and all of the various other "natural" elements. This suggests that these elements may not be so foreign to architecture as is typically assumed. This is to say, matter, as it is understood within the disciplines of biology and the natural sciences, is relevant for architecture as well.

Historically, the role of matter in architecture has been secondary to that of organization, its shape beholden to underlying and essential diagrams. For us, there is no pre-existing diagrammatic condition. This is true at both the methodological and the morphological levels. Matter, more conventionally termed "material" or "building material," typically did not enter into the design process until an organization had been generated to which it could then respond. An organization existed on the higher plane of ideas, disengaged from the base condition of matter. This relationship between matter and the organizations it expresses holds true for most approaches to the generation of architectural form, including various modes of classical, modernist, and postmodern composition.

Recently we have begun to see a shift away from this model, toward one in which matter is liberated. This new model results from the comingling of three separate areas of thought. The first comes from the realm of the natural sciences, in which complexity and irreversibility are increasingly understood as the engines of creation. Here, matter and the flows of energy it regulates is the foundation for larger organizations that, prior to their emergence in actual time and space did not exist in some prior space of ideation. The second comes from the realm of philosophy, as an appreciation for the poststructuralist challenge to signification increasingly dismantles architecture's reliance upon signs and references. The third comes from the realm of technology, in which the expanding role of computation in all phases of design inevitably changes the way we conceive and construct architecture. Advanced modeling and visualization applications allow for increasingly realistic simulation and exploration of the dynamics of material behavior. It is now possible to create entirely new materialities no longer confined by the limited set of behavioral characteristics embodied in traditional building materials. This new model posits matter as organizer. Diagrams and their progeny, organizations, are secondary and emergent, culled from the play of matter and energy in space and time. Matter first, organization second.

Interestingly, it is within the discipline of architecture that this model has taken shape. Perhaps this is due to our discipline's capacity for the incorporation and reorganization of the external, or perhaps we are simply at the right place at the right time. Whichever the case, a methodological model in which material dynamics generates architectural form promises an age of proliferation and abundance, for the organizations of matter never cease to unfold. Such a model will elaborate on ways by which matter and material dynamics may be understood and harnessed during the design process to provoke new organizations of form, program, effects, and events.

TECHNIQUE

Do-it-
yourself

1. Greg Lynn

Technique: the technology of design.

2. Mark Goulthorpe
I don't think of technology as technique.

3. Ben van Berkel and Peter Trümmer
Research, techniques and effects are the three steps that will always be central to architecture.

4. Achim Menges
A conditioned-based approach involves generative feedback between digital and physical form finding, structural analysis and ecological techniques.

5. Frank Gehry
Water and crinkled-up paper: they're just another form of decoration in my opinion; in a way, it is baroque.

6. Johan Bettum
In the last instance, technique is nothing more than the exfoliation of a style in the production of architecture.

7. François Burkhardt
Design is now concerned with the technique of differentiation, which implies a procedure with absolutely no rational basis in technology.

8. Peter Eisenman
The design of negatives, that is, both presence and absence, and the reversal of symmetries and asymmetries are Mies's signature.

9. MVRDV
Its web of possibilities—both economical and spatial—seems so complex that statistical techniques seem the only way to grasp its processes.

10. Otto Wagner
The aping of unsymmetrical buildings or the intentional making of an unsymmetrical composition in order to achieve a supposed painterly effect is totally objectionable.

11. Sanford Kwinter
Mood is always production and disequilibrium, a setting of the world into motion, the connection of a quiescent vortex to a new and unknown one.

12. Michael Hensel
Here the notion of the exotic comes into play. It refers to the unfamiliarity of shifts in patterns of appearance and behaviour, the capricious and divergent actualisation of transitory states.

13. Alejandro Zaera-Polo
We are interested in exploring the processes of construction and engineering on a variety of levels, rather than creating structures that are the simple implementation of an idea, or merely the scaffolding of an image.

14. Stan Allen
Landscape corridors are pathways for information exchange. Patches and corridors form larger networks of nodes and paths that allow communication, interaction and adaptation. This idea links landscape to infrastructure and information design through a logic of connectivity and feedback.

15. John Thackara
Today, design is promoted not as a force for good, but as a neutral tool to be used by technicians in the planning of complex urban environments, the harnessing to profitable use of technology, and the communication of information by visual or other means.

16. Rem Koolhaas
Compositionally it was simply an opportunistic infiltration of the island's residual space; into every gap and every slit and every available space we pushed programs with minimal containment, minimal cover, minimal articulation of mass to generate the greatest possible density with the least possible permanence.

17. Sulan Kolatan

Profiles of everyday domestic objects were cross-referenced according to their similarities and affinities. This was done in terms of morphology, performance, scale, programme, process-base and time (cross-categorical relationships). This ambivalence towards form and programme as relational constructs provides for the possibilities of appropriating, adapting and adopting these structures for the particular needs and desires of the inhabitants.

18. R. E. Somol

The prosaic technical and social facts of mass customization and consumer behavior are not adequate responses to the conceptual and material opportunities and impasses opened by arguments such as those found in Deleuze's *Difference and Repetition*. Architects who use these epiphenomena as an end state vision are simply promoting an infantilization of participation under the alibi of a much richer social and political thought.

19. R. E. Somol

While some today are preoccupied by process, technique and genealogy, I am interested in polemic and effect. I realize that when you're in the academic milieu, you have to simulate the rigor of process, indexicality, and technique, but the stakes that I find in our practice are different than the ones that I think are necessary (although not sufficient) to teach in an academic institution.

20. Jason Payne

Techniques often slip out from under whatever material organizations they are driving, though techniques are not like concepts which can usually be entirely divorced from one set of forms and relocated in another. Techniques, having arisen out of the material and formal specificity of their host organizations, never entirely shake off their original uses, behaviors, effects, and sensibilities. This makes technique a device most useful in organizational and even disciplinary exchange.

21. Jean Baudrillard

Beyond "style" and its caricatured version in "styling," the commercial kitsch of the nineteenth century and the modern style, the Bauhaus projects the basis of a rational conception of environmental totality for the first time. Beyond the genres (architecture, painting, furnishings, etc.), beyond "art" and its academic sanction, it extends the aesthetic to the entire everyday world; at the same time it is all of technique in the service of everyday life.

22. Ali Rahim

Contemporary design techniques are temporal, process-driven methods that provide new transformative effects in cultural, social and political production. Such a technique acts on or influences an object, which in turn modifies human behaviors and technical performance . . . Contemporary techniques are organised and guided by probabilities, which are unlimited and allow for the production of performative effects in architecture. Moreover, contemporary techniques are destabilised by temporally located potentials that make possible the development of new organisations.

23. Michael Bell

Technique recalls two major voices: Michel Foucault and Lewis Mumford. Foucault's explication of historic techniques rather than forms is in "in the water" we all drink. From Morphosis' 2,4,6 House to Asymptope's chronologies or the CAT-Scan sectioning of Alias and Maya models, we have began using infinitely small, often arcane, notations of actual and simulated techniques. Neil Denari's work describes an (urban) architecture of accumulated techniques: distributed systems that nonetheless have local architectural effect.

24. Neil Denari

Today there are no ideas, only techniques. If ideas were previously executed through a set of conventional techniques, contemporary culture now has methods that have yet to be matched with ideas. They have substantially supplanted autonomous conceptual thinking (idea to form via a technical process) with a new regime of content-making tools. But rather than "it's all in the software," or "the author is dead, now we just have systems analysts," the control of work is now found in the organization of techniques more than in the a priori establishment of ideas: techniques are ideas. As they rewrite the rules by which architecture is made, they will eventually become subject to the question "Why do it?" instead of the directive "Just use it." When this happens, architecture will have advanced to a more complex medium than ever before. In the meantime, techniques give us means to effect change.

TECHNIQUE

25. Mark Lee

Residence Assistants at Harvard have to follow three simple rules when alone in a dormitory room with a student of the opposite sex:

1. A light bulb of minimum 60-watts must be turned on.
2. The door must be open a minimum of 90 degrees.
3. A minimum of three feet must be touching the ground simultaneously.

These rules share the common goal of preventing inappropriate behavior between assistant and student, but differ in their operative techniques. The first two are matters of cultural policy. They are negotiable according to customs and habits (i.e., privacy and modesty are negligible if the subjects are exhibitionists). The third rule, broaching on specifics of mechanics and performance, is a matter of instrumentality.

In architecture, the distinction between cultural policies and instrumentality has become increasingly blurred in the last two decades. With the proliferation of design technologies coinciding with the expansion of cultural obligations, architects are faced with the predicament of having an excess of means to achieve increasingly broadened yet undefined goals. As the speed in developing these technologies surpasses the speed in developing their feasibility and implementation, the supply of techniques exceeds cultural demand.

One symptom of this deflation is a feverish feedback loop, where cultural policies and instrumentality become interdependent. On one hand, architects are becoming beguiled by techniques that provide answers before significant questions can be formulated. On the other, the provocation of attributing meaning to the question "how" or confounding performance to the question "why" is being met with diminishing returns within the critical establishment.

The persistence of this feedback loop, möbius in its nature, will inevitably result in another form of autonomy, further deflating the discipline of architecture from a position of relevance within the larger cultural discourse. With architecture's incurable desire to assume responsibility in response to the latest categories of cultural criticism, the understanding of technique's role as a "means of achieving one's purposes," needs to be redefined in light of the constantly shifting territories of both the means and the purposes.

An examination of OMA's production of techniques in the last fifteen years provides a projective model to reconcile this tension between cultural policies and instrumentality. The techniques could be divided into two basic strains—those which address general conditions such as Bigness, Congestion, Generic, No-details, and those which operate on specifics such as Voiding, Stacking, Ramping, Juxtaposing. One embodies attitude and establishes groundwork, the other embraces specificities and promotes development. One speculates on intentionalities and prerequisites, the other exacerbates effects and form. The two are not freely interchangeable, but discriminately conflate to engender an architectural paradigm. This model of projective delineation between cultural policies and instrumentality frees design production from the self-serving feedback loop and provides a renewed relevance for the understanding of means and purposes, proving that in architecture at least, technique is more important than size.

...makes
perfect

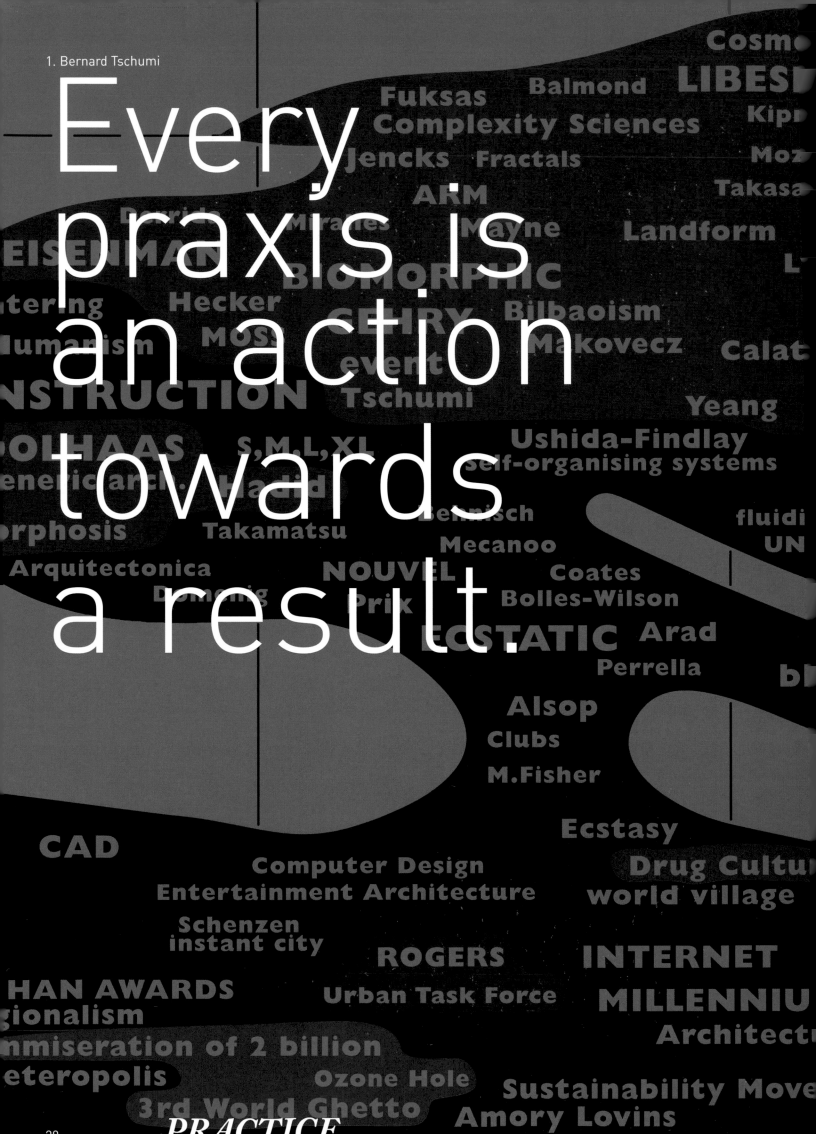

Every praxis is an action towards a result.

Cosmo
LIBES
Fuksas   Balmond   Kipr
Complexity Sciences
Jencks   Fractals   Moz
Takasa
ARM   Mayne   Landform
L
EISE   BIOMORPHIC
ering   Hecker   GEHRY   Bilbaoism
Humanism   MOS   Makovecz   Calat
event
NSTRUCTION   Tschumi   Yeang
OLHAAS   S, M, L, XL   Ushida-Findlay
self-organising systems
rphosis   Takamatsu   Behnisch   fluidi
Mecanoo   UN
Arquitectonica   NOUVEL   Coates
Prix   Bolles-Wilson
a result.   ECSTATIC   Arad
Perrella   bl
Alsop
Clubs
M.Fisher
Ecstasy
CAD   Drug Cultur
Computer Design   world village
Entertainment Architecture
Schenzen
instant city
ROGERS   INTERNET
HAN AWARDS   MILLENNIU
gionalism   Urban Task Force   Architect
nmiseration of 2 billion
eteropolis   Ozone Hole   Sustainability Move
3rd World Ghetto   Amory Lovins
leisure culture   *PRACTICE*   NATURAL CAPITALISM

2. MVRDV
For us, the combination of practice and research is indispensable.

3. Mark Wigley
Gropius effectively turned design into a form of management, with the architect as "coordinator."

4. Michael Hensel, Michael Weinstock, Achim Menges
Emergence does not await a practice and defies conventional categorisation as either theory or practice.

5. Cecil Balmond
Rem seemed to be someone with an open agenda, highly speculative and aggressive about the contemporary condition.

6. Steven Johnson
A new kind of hybrid has appeared—a fusion of artist, programmer, and complexity theorist—creating interactive projects.

7. Michael Sorkin
For Gehry, the computer is a tool, not a partner—an instrument for catching the curve, not for inventing it.

8. Frank Gehry
The new computer and management system allows us to unite all the players—the contractor, the engineer, the architect—with one modeling system.

9. Sylvia Lavin
Modernity is . . . an inconsistent phenomenon, riddled by moments of oscillation that have opened architecture to spaces of significant experimentation and that have demanded extraordinary agility.

10. Johan Bettum
Theory and practice have no relevance without each other, nor indeed do they ever stand alone. Where one is frivolous, the other resists and discerns, and vice versa.

11. Jonathan Hill
The architect and user are not distinct and separate entities, necessarily antagonistic towards each other, but exist within each other: the user being an (illegal) architect.

12. R. E. Somol
Practices first solicit precedents and then try to distinguish themselves from them. This is the way professions establish authority: by simultaneously generating acts of nostalgia and amnesia.

13. Stan Allen
Field conditions intentionally mixes high theory with low practices. The assumption here is that architectural theory does not arise in a vacuum, but always in a complex dialogue with practical work.

14. Polly Apfelbaum
I considered myself a hybrid and also a poacher, so anything was up for grabs. I started poaching because I really wanted to take from as many worlds as possible.

15. Paul Virilio
Constructed space now occurs within an electronic topology, where the framing of the point of view and the scan lines of numerical images give new form to the practice of mapping.

16. Bruce Mau
We are interested in recuperating and reinvesting the term "life style" so that it speaks of the designer's role in shaping the lives we lead and the world in which we live.

17. Bernard Tschumi
The *Transcripts* offer a different reading of architecture in which space, movement and events are ultimately independent, yet stand in a new relation to one another, so that the conventional components of architecture are broken down and rebuilt along different axes.

18. Mark Cousins
I am suggesting that there may be what we might call "weak disciplines," which does not of course make them weak. It means that the public, visible part of the curriculum . . . none-the-less does very little to define the nature of the practice.

19. Servo
Servo motors translate digital code into machinic processes. They behave principally as enablers that allow two distinct languages to converse and interact. For Servo, this has been the primary way in which we have constructed and considered the practice of our collaborative.

20. Frederick Kiesler
I designed the spatial configuration. I invited the painters Duchamp, Max Ernst, Matta, Miró, Tanguy, and the sculptors Hare and Maria to carry out my plan. They collaborated with fervour. I conceived each part of the whole, form and content, specially for each artist.

21. Alejandro Zaera-Polo and Farshid Moussavi
We have tried to put the emphasis of our practice on the architectural construct, on the materiality of the project, and on its organizational qualities. Geometry, construction, organization, materiality, technique, and pragmatics have become an alternative to a temporary suspension of the exclusivity of cultural analysis.

22. Craig Hodgetts
Practice is a concept due for rehab. The AIA is the organizational equivalent of cement overshoes and is just as likely to carry the architectural profession to the bottom of the stream. Where are the brands, the I.T. systems, the multitasking, the material innovations, the media, the samples, the hybrids, the mobility, the grit, and the bling-bling?

23. Helene Furján
Practice, as the format or terrain of architectural intervention and invention, is no longer singular but plural, no longer about propriety (the proper place of the architect or the proper rules of the game): practices are tactical operations, multiple, diverse, and competitive, operations that together transform, deform, contest, and define the discipline and its spaces of effects.

24. Walter Gropius
The Bauhaus strives to bring together all creative effort into one whole, to reunify all the disciplines of practical art—sculpture, painting, handicrafts, and the crafts—as inseparable components of a new architecture. The ultimate, if distant, aim of the Bauhaus is the unified work of art—the great structure—in which there is no distinction between monumental and decorative art.

25. Sanford Kwinter
BMD developed a practice that became at once increasingly collaborative and independent of the client. Collaborative because "through-design" meant reengineering the impetus by first designing (rethinking) the client's task itself; independent, because a fully confident set of social researches was forming within the BMD milieu, a constant interrogation of "what is possible?" and "how can this be put at the service . . . of life?"

26. Mark Goulthorpe
If you want to attain a change in modes of receptivity, you won't do it by operating within an extant mode of creativity. You have to rethink your creative mode of practice, and if we're going to exploit the potential of computers, it will not be through the extension of current modes of thought but by entirely reinventing the creative circuits through which we conceive these projects.

27. Michael Bell
After being exacerbated by the material and production systems of high-end commodities such as automobiles and fossil fuels, architectural practice is regaining agency and effectiveness. Is it possible that a generation forty years from now will see this time as the decade when architects engaged all those modes of power that were assumed to have eclipsed the territorial goals of small-scale practices—and by "small scale" I mean even SOM and Renzo Piano—that sought to construct territory in the small-scale territories of an architectural office and a local site, and without large realms of research or design capitalization.

28. Jesse Reiser
Foucault was succinct on this point: "I do not think that there is anything that is functional—by its very nature, liberating. Liberty is a practice."

It is irresponsible to assume that architecture can or should aspire to do things that are better accomplished through action and legislation. People have a tendency to confuse material constructs for the practices that take place in them. There is a certain agreement we have that when we walk into an office, we will work. On an ultimate level there is no material compulsion to conform in that way. On a practical level, one could do anything in a restaurant, in the office, even though 99 percent of us behave otherwise.

PRACTICE

29. David Salomon

Common to the different definitions of "practice" is the theme of plurality. Practice is a recurring, even habitual, occurrence—one is never enough. The aim of these seemingly compulsive acts has ordinarily been refinement and conformity. These ends are to be achieved by parsing scores, scripts, game plans, buildings, etc., into discrete parts and techniques, which, once isolated, are examined and repeated until they could be reproduced automatically. In these terms, the function of "practice" is nothing less than the elimination of difference and risk. It is, after all, what makes "perfect."

The perfect, if not stagnant state practice, is thus consistent with the conventional view of architectural practice, a term that defines both firms and the particular operations performed therein. For both definitions, the primary goal is to efficiently produce designs and drawings that in turn can be used to build buildings. The professional emphasis on working things out and solving problems before they occur suggests that what typically takes place in architectural offices is closer to a synonym of practice, namely, rehearsal. That is, the tasks performed in private are done in the preparation of a public performance for the benefit of others—in architecture, the building and client respectively. Thus, despite the fact that a practicing architect is typically defined as one who "builds," in fact he never does, but only "rehearses" the building.

The rote and pragmatic nature of architectural practice, then, is not where one would expect to expand architecture's disciplinary reach. Yet, today, a number of architects, by exploiting practice's inherent plurality, have recognized its potentially generative, even speculative, possibilities. Rather than seeing it as preparation for something else, or as a series of standardized and routinized acts, its repetitive nature is coveted for its potential to produce difference and complexity rather than identicality and conformity. Although abandoning the earlier generation's insistence on resisting or opposing the infiltration of external cultural forces, it builds on the previous moment's critical inquiries that expanded the definition of architecture to include discursive as well as material operations. Thus, it can easily engage and incorporate a variety of practices—spatial, political, social, economic, as well as formal—into both its processes and ultimately its buildings.

Bolstered by digital technology's sublime image making ability, and enabled by its information processing and communication capacities, these new practitioners of architecture are expanding the boundaries of design expertise beyond the modernist poles of aesthetic and/or technical mastery. No longer searching for standardized solutions, the otherwise divergent practices of OMA/AMO, Bernard Cache, Greg Lynn, MVRDV, Stan Allen, Neil Denari, and even Frank Gehry, have in their own way reconceptualized their practice(s) to support constant experimenting, adjusting, hypothesizing, and testing. The practicing of architecture can thus become more improvisational than inhibiting; less a pragmatic mechanism of perfecting than a knowledge-producing machine. Clearly, "practice" isn't over yet, but the game has already begun.

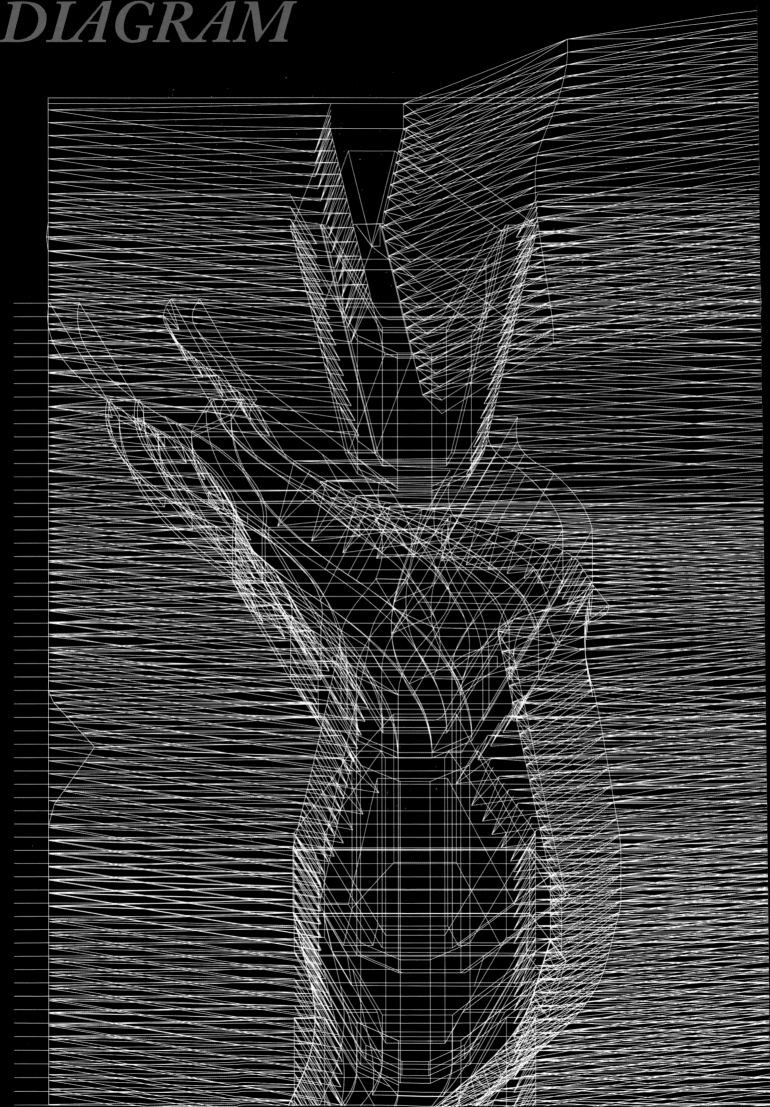

DIAGRAM

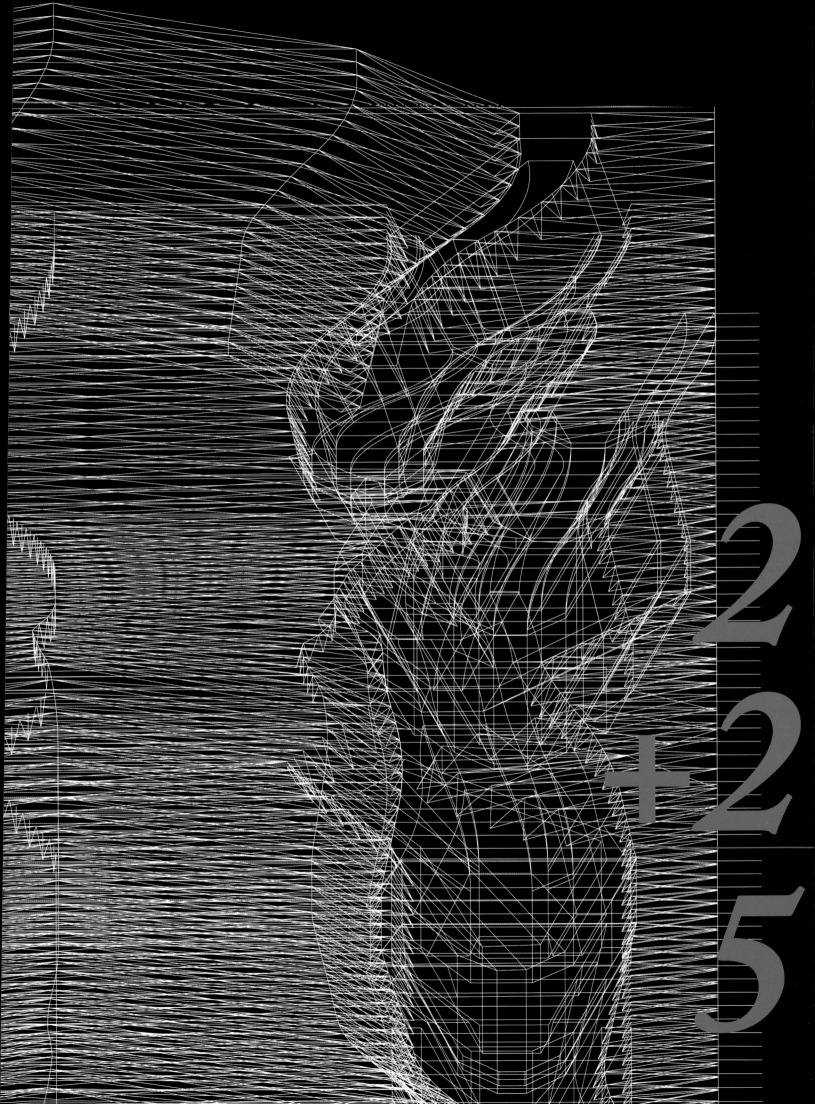

Every diagram is a spacio-temporal multiplicity.

2. Ben van Berkel and Peter Trümmer
The proliferating, generating and open system of diagrammatical instrumentalization.

3. Pia Ednie-Brown
Elusive, textural figments that seemed to speak in passing through mutating patternings across which almost unspeakable sensibilities passed.

4. Le Corbusier
Having discovered the law of the "Modulor," we had to think of its possible uses and therefore also of its material form.

5. MVRDV
By selecting or connecting data according to hypothetical prescriptions, a world of numbers turns into diagrams.

6. Cecil Balmond
It is not ad hocism, which is collage, but a methodology of evolving starting points that, by emergence, creates its own series of orders.

7. Toyo Ito
A building is ultimately the equivalent of the diagram of the space used to abstractedly describe the mundane activities presupposed by the structure.

8. Manuel De Landa
True thinking consists in *problem-posing*, that is, in framing the right problems rather than solving them. It is only through skillful problem-posing that we can begin to think diagrammatically.

9. Jeffrey Kipnis
Yet, in each and every case, the erotics of the object—that cocktail of desire, revulsion, and fear it stirs—is an *index* of the transformation of matter by information through force toward effect.

10. Albert Pope
It is apparent that the grid is not only an icon of order; it is also a benign apparatus capable of bringing out of an undifferentiated flux an inclusive, heterogeneous field of almost unlimited complexity.

11. Stan Allen
A diagram architecture is part of a new sensibility characterized by a disinterest in the allied projects of critique or the production of meaning, preferring instead immediacy, dryness, and the pleasures of the literal.

12. Rem Koolhaas
Maybe, architecture doesn't have to be stupid after all. Liberated from the obligation to construct, it can become a way of thinking about anything—a discipline that represents relationships, proportions, connections, effects, the diagram of everything.

13. Michael Sorkin
The circulation loop that organizes the building sites within Opus recapitulates the highway loop that arrays Opus and other fringe developments around cities like Minneapolis and Atlanta. The order is centrifugal, about perimeters rather than centers, a logic of dispersion.

14. Andrew Benjamin
Once freed from the need to represent, the line and the diagram work as ends in themselves. This is not intended to preclude pragmatic necessities; rather, it is to allow for the emergence of the diagram as a plot to a complexity—a complex of relations—that is always more than the addition of elements.

15. Margaret Crawford
If a map of their efforts were to be drawn, it would reveal a continent covered by a wildly uneven pattern of overlapping circles representing mall-catchment areas, each circle's size and location dictated by demographic surveys measuring income levels and purchasing power. In a strangely inverted version of central-place theory, developers identified areas where consumer demand was not being met and where malls could fill the commercial voids.

16. R. E. Somol

The success of the indexical, beautifully if informally evidenced in the automatic procedures provided by the computer, emerges as the apotheosis of criticality, with its related emphasis on representation, process, narrativity, difficulty, interpretation, and the simulated real. It now remains to be seen whether it is possible to develop a projective pedagogy of the diagrammatic with its own set of correlates: performance, effect, plasticity, ease, experimentation, and real virtuality.

17. Jesse Reiser

As architects we are apt to regard diagramming in terms of either the fixed norms of classical geometry and typology or as reductive descriptions of programmatic or functional relations (bubble diagramming). If, however, we shift our focus from such static models to dynamical (essentially time-based) systems then an entirely new horizon of possibilities emerges ... A corresponding shift, therefore, is necessary from the fixed, bounded geometry of classicism to a language of waves, fields and fronts.

18. Sanford Kwinter

In Boccioni's *Stati d'animo* series, what we find depicted are three evental complexes, or *three morphogenetic fields*, each arising within the same complex system of real matter and forces. Their startling morphological variety can be accounted for by the fact that each is triggered by a different singularity that, in turn, binds it to a specific attractor—*farewells*: turbulence, aggregation; *parting*: bifurcation, decelension; *staying*: inertia, laminarity. The inchoate qualities of the form "fragments" that traditionally we are conditioned to see here are, in fact, nothing else than the manifest work of time plying the folds of matter to release the virtual forms within it ... A unique field of unfolding, a section through a distinct epigenetic landscape in which forms exist only in evolution or equilibrium, that is, as event-generated *diagrams*.

19. Gilles Deleuze and Félix Guattari

A diagram has neither substance nor form, neither content nor expression ... *Diagrams* must be distinguished from *indexes*, which are territorial signs, but also from *icons*, which pertain to reterritorialization, and from *symbols*, which pertain to relative or negative deterritorialization. Defined diagrammatically in this way, an abstract machine is neither an infrastructure that is determining in the last instance nor a transcendental Idea that is determining in the supreme instance. Rather, it plays a piloting role. The diagrammatic or abstract machine does not function to represent, even something real, but rather constructs a real that is yet to come, a new type of reality.

20. Alejandro Zaera-Polo

One of the great potentials of diagrams, statistics, notations, and all the tools of abstraction that come together with informational technology is that they allow us to produce alienation within reality, without having to resort to a discourse external to the discipline. Alienation is a powerful instrument for producing new architectural possibilities. It provides the capacity for a constant displacement from a closed state of conventions or orders, and the possibility of triggering virtualities in a project, generally excluded by a historical construction of tools or responses. Practices of alienation in architecture were extensively explored in the 1980s, destabilizing the object by resorting to other disciplines, or destabilizing the subject by embracing automatism, randomness, or chaos. We are interested in notating and organizing reality in which both the subject and the object of architecture are mediated, so that the output of the process is not predetermined, a priori, in relation to existing models or conventions, does not require abandoning the disciplinary field, nor declining authorship. Pragmatic considerations are therefore not opposed to the exploration of the virtual.

The potential of diagrams and information technology as medium is not the capacity to produce virtual immaterial worlds, but rather the possibility of synthesizing new materials and working with them with a rigor not possible before the appearance of these tools. We are not interested in virtual architecture, but in the virtual in architecture. Critical architecture is not generated through a theoretical discourse that later materializes. This discipline's specificity demands that we work with materials that have geometries, organizations, properties, and so on. Materiality is ultimately the necessary condition of architecture, the diagram of the instrument that permits us to construct new composite materials. Diagrams and abstractions allow us to synthesize new materials and develop the project as a process of material transformation, rather than translating a theoretical discourse into architecture.

DIAGRAM

21. Ben van Berkel and Caroline Bos

For the last eight years or so much architectural production has focused on diagrams to define new planning strategies for architecture and urban design. Diagramming has turned into a major discourse in architectural theory. What has remained underexposed, however, is the process by which diagrams are abstracted, instrumentalized, or otherwise manipulated in such a way that they can be filled with architectural meaning. That is to say, they can become structural, can be programmed, or can be made to point to specific architectural qualities. It is this process that intrigues us more and more. When a diagram switches meaning (when, for instance, the mathematical scheme of the Klein Bottle reveals itself as a seamless environment of mobility and exchange), it is like waking up to a new world—how do we fall from one world into the next?

Diagrams typically condense information. In our practice we have generated diagrams that (re)define urban structures as sites of mobility, and programs as places of popular access. Those diagrams are intended to show what is actually happening on a location, uncluttered by presumptions about issues as high-minded as ideological representation or as banal as square footage and building typologies.

Increasingly, diagrams also incorporate the effects of the interaction between different actors. Recent diagrams have brought forward new ways to define user categories in relation to territorial and time-based parameters, thus managing to articulate hard parameters, real workable architectural ingredients out of the soft notion of flow. Flow has ceased to be an amorphous mass but is broken down into programmatic elements and constraints that can be used to make architecture. This relational approach to diagramming generates new insights into the developmental potentials of locations in an integral manner.

A frequently asked question (or critique) about diagrams is whether they really are design tools, or are primarily communicational devices. In our own practice, they are both often used to qualify information in such a way that a problem, or a central question at the core of the design, is elucidated. But at the same time, diagramming reveals something else: a second hidden reality that exists parallel to the first more obvious reality. In recent years we have explored different fields with our students, varying from industrial design to business practices and art, all the time in search of that surprising moment when the diagram reveals its second nature.

Looked at like this, we wonder if the diagram is not in fact a figment—something which, like a ghost, exists outside normal reality, but which nonetheless, as an imaginary construct, is real. The reality of the figment is fuller than that of a concept, idea, or notion, which is vague, mostly verbally articulated, and flat. Figments, on the other hand, have a whole history; they move from narrative to narrative, and they act and interact in explicit forms, thus moving fluently between the realms of the representational and the actual. An analogous effect is achieved by programming a camera to click on automatically. The image that results is partly generated by the framing of the previous conscious instant, partly by the unexpected and uncontrollable behavior of the ingredients framed in that instant, and partly by the automatic mechanism of the camera. The unplanned effects of automatism together with the duplicity of the visual make you fall from one world into the next.

EXTREME FORM

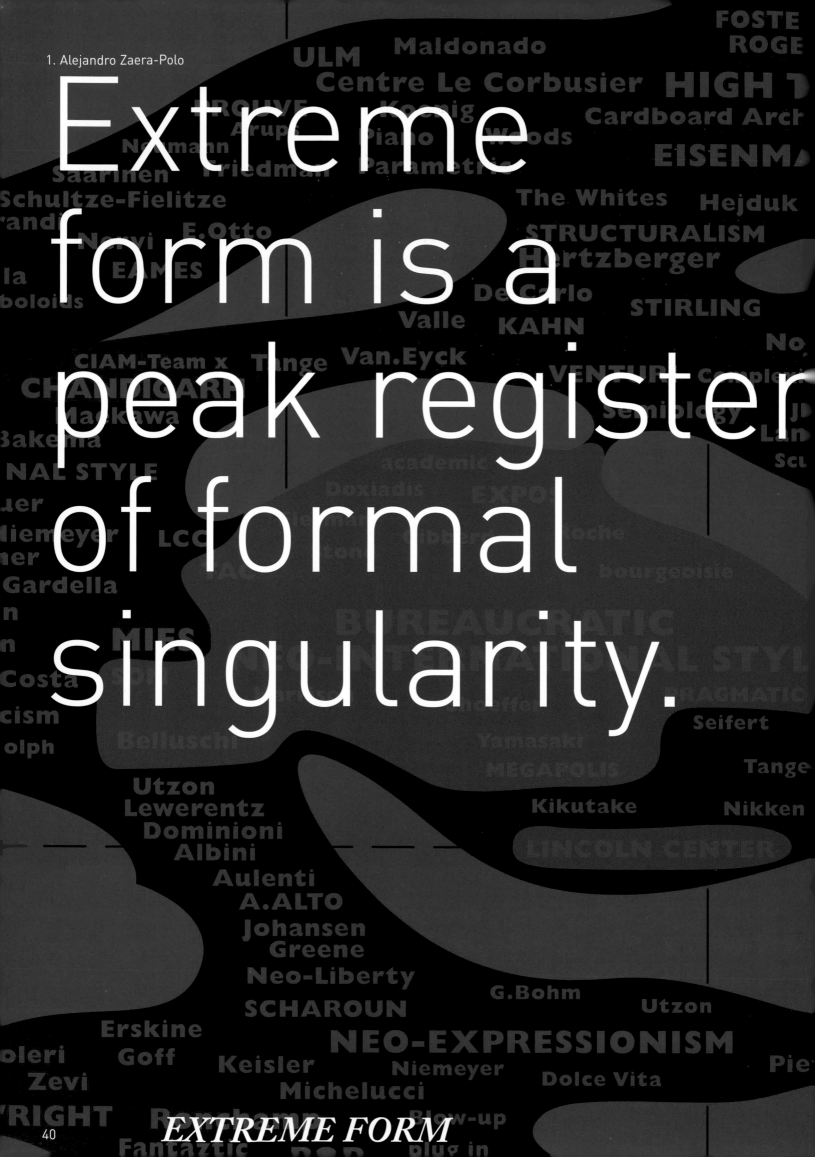

1. Alejandro Zaera-Polo

Extreme form is a peak register of formal singularity.

EXTREME FORM

2. Jeffrey Kipnis

Furthermore, it must be an architecture, i.e., a proposal of principles (though not prescriptions) for design. Finally, it must experiment with and project new forms.

3. Sanford Kwinter

The *dynamical* theory of morphogenesis, which characterizes all form as the irruption of a discontinuity, not *on* the system but *in* it or *of* it.

4. Greg Lynn

Many blobs of all different sizes and shapes and irreducible typological essences. Blobs that threaten to overrun a terrorized and deterritorialized tectonics like a bad B movie.

5. Hugh Ferriss

Designers have generally come to realize the importance of the principle stated by the late Louis Sullivan, "Form follows Function." The axiom is not weakened by the further realization that Effect follows Form.

6. René Thom

To define the spatial form of an animal, for example, is equivalent to defining what is called in biology the phenotype of this animal, and nothing is more difficult to define exactly.

7. Ellen Lupton

David Cronenberg's *Videodrome* (1983) conjoins the body and machinery in reverse: here, inanimate objects pulse with life. First a videocassette, then a television and VCR, swell, buckle, and moan, their plastic surfaces heaving with morbid sexuality.

8. Lars Lerup

Shaped like the whacked-out species of an exotic aquarium—huge partially disintegrated flounders, schools of drunken piranhas, bloated whales— slow, fast, frazzled, mostly opaque, and surrounded by wisps of indecisive grayish-brown mists, clouds often operate in opposite directions.

9. Sulan Kolatan

We prefer to think in terms of extreme range rather than extreme form. In "housings," extreme form is but one instance within an extreme range of chimeric variation that touches all bases including and between the extreme and the normative.

10. Michael Hensel

Form finding is a design method that deploys and instrumentalises the self-organisation of material systems under the influence of extrinsic forces. The question is then: How can we approach form finding if material form continuously transmutes in response to an equally dynamic force-context?

11. Clover Lee

The extreme implies a challenge to the norm. The fact is there is no criterion in form, but only accepted norms within the manufacturing and construction processes. The challenge is not in achieving extreme form, but in inventing extreme construction and fabrication techniques, where any form will be the norm.

12. Neil Leach

No longer is the architect the demiurgic formmaker of the past. The architect has been recast as the controller of processes, who oversees the "formation" of architecture. With the development of new computational techniques, we find ourselves on the threshold of a new paradigm for architecture—a paradigm in which "swarm tectonics" plays a crucial role.

13. Craig Hodgetts

Like its sibling in the world of sports, the identification of architecture as a frozen performance has led to an unprecedented appreciation for radical formal experiments, with a concurrent appetite for unusual materials, processes, and configurations. Even Gertrude Stein-like incomprehensibilities seem to sneak under the radar if the proposition promises sufficient bang for the buck.

14. Manuel De Landa

When one looks at current artistic results the most striking fact is that, once a few interesting forms have been generated, the evolutionary process seems to run out of possibilities ... This stands in sharp contrast to the incredible combinatorial productivity of natural forms like the thousands of original architectural "designs" exhibited by vertebrate or insect bodies.

15. Cecil Balmond

But cool new shapes and blobs are nothing more than mere façade if they are propped up by standard post and beam constructions. To create an integrity in the establishing of a free shape a new method is needed for configuration with flexible start points. Instead of line—surface; instead of equi-support—scatter; instead of fixed centre— a moving locus; and instead of points—zones.

16. Sylvia Lavin

Plasticity today obeys no conventional formal or semiological logic and instead exploits gaps in the discipline's stabilities to produce experimental sensibilities ... Its efficacy derives, first, from the fact that not only does plastic lack traditional material ethics but also from the fact that plasticity is an unsettling diagram of the negotiation between concept and materiality. Second, plasticity both constitutes and exceeds the modern, its fluid agility embodying an aim that modernity's obsession with structural and formal regulation repressed.

17. Johan Bettum

Extreme form in architecture is nothing but the absolute synthesis of unequal forms—social, cultural, and physical—that flow in and out of one another and charge the architectural object with a tension that at once bestows upon it the acuteness and excess that characterizes the "extreme." A physical form is merely an instance in an endless array of possible material forms, none more or less unique than any other. Architecture, whether dressed in Euclidean or non-Euclidean geometry, always exceeds this instance.

18. Gilles Deleuze and Félix Guattari

A line that delimits nothing, that describes no *contour*, that no longer goes from one point to another but instead passes between points, that is always declining from the horizontal and the vertical and deviating from the diagonal, that is constantly changing direction, a mutant line of this kind that is without outside or inside, form or background, beginning or end, and that is alive as a continuous variation—such a line is truly an abstract line, and describes a smooth space.

19. Charles Jencks

Extreme form is motivated by excess and symbolism, the desire in a Baroque age to over communicate and be heard and to say something important. "Weak form" has been seen as a natural consequence of weak belief in an age of lost narratives. Where architects have distanced themselves from a public language and credible content, they may oscillate between weak shapes and extreme form, believing in neither. Extreme form then becomes the hammer of architecture to beat the public into willing submission: Koolhaas's sadomasochistic Voluntary Prisoners of Architecture.

20. Michael Bell

After Sanford Kwinter's reference to extreme sports, and to a surfer who both describes and is described by a wave, in his essay "Flying the Bullet," students at Rice began to literally use extreme sports to produce extreme form. The term *extreme form* was simultaneously used to indicate an emergent form—an epigenetic landscape—and something that was sublimely beautiful. Its reliance on the word form is both fortunate and unfortunate: it links formalist criticism and phenomena with the emergent themes of extreme or crisis situations. It also suggests that, like extreme sports, our cultural production demands somewhat desperate acts of near-self-harm: that the new arrives on the cusp of crisis.

EXTREME FORM

21. Jason Payne

In 1977, scientists discovered an exotic new ecosystem at the bottom of the Galapagos Rift. There, where colonies of monstrous creatures thrive on toxic chemicals spewed into superheated water, they have discovered 300 new species, ninety new genera, twenty new families, and one new phylum. These animals cannot live in any other environment and their reproductive and evolutionary cycles are noticeably sped up. They live fast and die young. Improbable yet possible ecologies like this illustrate that even the strangest combinations of ingredients, combinations that from any angle would seem unproductive, can sometimes spawn interesting and viable results. So, too, might less apparent economies, technologies, materials, and desires—the allied elements that comingle to create architectural ecosystems—produce unforeseen built environments. Architecture need not be so much in service of the known as it is in affirmation of the new.

The term *extreme* means simply the relative distance from a mean, or norm, condition. *Extreme form*, then, describes form developed beyond the basic disposition in which it enters the world. If only our discourse would allow for such uncluttered definitions, we would have much more form at this moment of disciplinary evolution. Unfortunately this is not the case. The term *form* has become politicized to the degree that those designers who would prioritize its careful production are pushed hard to one end of an artificial spectrum, radicalized in their efforts. As a result, it often seems as if all form is extreme, making the term heading this section redundant. Ultimately, however, this understanding of form is ill-considered and unproductive. Leaving political definitions aside allows a movement toward an analytical and more positive use of the term *extreme form*.

To find the extreme we first must locate the mean. There are two general models for establishing mean formal conditions: the historical and the systemic. A historical model asserts that formal norms are those that have evolved over time to become persistent, or recurrent, thereby taking on familiarity. These norms also include form rarely seen in contemporary practice, having achieved familiarity at some earlier historical moment and persisting now as artifact. An extreme form within this model would be anything not previously seen or known no matter what its level of morphological development may be.

Conversely, a systemic model for the evaluation of form is a-historical, relying not on precedent but rather on degree of morphological sophistication, or refinement. It is not that forms measured within this model are without their own developmental history but rather that their normality and extremity are not evaluated based on cultural history. Refined form is what has been worked on more, contains more layers, and is more multivalent. It is not necessarily more complex morphologically, because sometimes the refinement aims toward formal simplicity. There is also no particular idiomatic affiliation with extreme form, though clearly those practices and movements most committed to the active role of form in design and in life tend to achieve higher levels of refinement, hence more extreme form.

Ultimately a healthy coordination of both the historical and the systemic model leads to more successful form, extreme or otherwise. In the same way Nietzsche advocates the careful mixture of three distinct approaches to history in his essay "On the Use and Abuse of History for Life," so, too, can these two models be used selectively for the refinement of form. This requires calibrated and disproportionate attention to each, however, due to the hegemony of the historical model and the expertise required for access to the second. The historical model is nearly automatic in its expression of norms due to their persistence and familiarity. For this reason, culturally familiar forms cannot be ignored. However, known forms can become too familiar, obscuring their innate systemic potential as well as giving the mistaken impression that certain unfamiliar forms are extreme when they are in fact simply new arrivals. Meanwhile, systemically extreme forms go undeveloped for lack of attention. Happily we are currently living in a time of decreasing trust in the historical value of things while simultaneously increasing our technical, material, and aesthetic expertise in the production of form.

LANDSCAPE

Landscape with figures and gadgets.

LANDSCAPE

2. John Muir
The whole landscape showed design.

3. Russell Fortmeyer
Landscape is a temporal surface for operation.

4. Gordon Cullen
A city is a dramatic event in the environment.

5. J. B. Jackson
Why is it, I wonder, that we have trouble agreeing
on the meaning of *landscape*?

6. Rem Koolhaas, Bruce Mau, Petra Blaisse, et al.
Tree city is a diagram designed to maximize the
park's options for survival.

7. Robert Venturi, Denise Scott Brown, Steven Izenour
To move through this landscape is to move over
vast expansive texture: the megatexture of the
commercial landscape.

8. Michael Sorkin
At its core, the greenhouse—or Disneyland—
offers a view of alien nature, edited, a better version, a kind of sublime.

9. Michael Hensel
Landscape urbanism . . . entails a shift in emphasis
from the figure-ground composition of urban fabric towards conceiving urban surface as a generative field.

10. Sanford Kwinter
The epigenetic landscape . . . is only a template, or
virtual form, assembled *in another dimension*, as
a multiplicity generated by an extremely complex
field of forces.

11. Celebration Pattern Book
No more than two different species of canopy
trees, two different species of ornamental trees,
five different species of shrubs or hedges, and
four different species of ground covers.

12. Jean Baudrillard
It is useless to seek to strip the desert of its cinematic aspects in order to restore its original
essence; those features are thoroughly superim-
posed upon it and will not go away.

13. Paul Goldberger
There is no better place to think about the
American landscape and what it is turning
into than here, in Orange County, where brand-
new suburbs sprawl across the land with such
intensity that Los Angeles, by comparison,
seems almost an old-fashioned, traditional city.

14. Roberto Burle Marx
A garden is a complex of aesthetic and plastic
intentions; and the plant is, to a landscape artist,
not only a plant—rare, unusual, ordinary or
doomed to disappearance—but it is also a color,
a shape, a volume, or an arabesque in itself.

15. Alex Wall
The term *landscape* no longer refers to prospects
of pastoral innocence but rather invokes the functioning matrix of connective tissue that organizes
not only objects and spaces but also the dynamic
processes and events that move through them.
This is landscape as active surface, structuring the
conditions for new relationships and interactions
among the things it supports.

16. Cecil Balmond
Landscape, urbanscape, building scapes can all be thought of as "infoscape"... Once those connections are made, it becomes evident to me that what is possible is a much broader coalition, of generic processes that involve the same layer of information, working at different scales, connected by inner hierarchies of logic. Ultimately it is about the serial orders of pattern.

17. The Center for Land Use Interpretation
Another architecture is rising in the expanded landscape of preparedness. Condensed simulacrum of our existing urban environments are forming within our communities, where the first responders to emergencies, on a smaller scale, practice their craft of dealing with disaster. The scenario grounds of emergency training include mock hazardous material spills, train wrecks, building collapse, fires, and debris-strewn landscapes...

18. Keller Easterling
For so many strata of culture—from geology to network architecture to urbanism to globalization—landscape is diagram. Like a diagram, it requires no representation. Like a diagram, it has temporal parameters. Like a diagram, it is not reliant on any single artefact but rather continues to produce artifacts in time. It is an organization that is always becoming.

19. Detlef Mertins
Formally compelling, the Downsview projects are more significant for demonstrating a new conception of design, focusing on practices and techniques that invest matter with intelligence, animation and potential. Reshaping and redirecting, deleting and inserting, seeding and planting, structuring and unstructuring, separating and mixing, mutating and accelerating, are all procedures in landscape design geared towards the production of certain effects while monitoring changes that occur within the environment.

20. Mohsen Mostafavi
As a framework for the imagination, landscape produces new insights in response to the contemporary urban situation. It allows one to describe that territory in terms of an equal, although artificial, dialogue between buildings and landscapes. Yet this dialogue is not limited by the traditional definition of the terms "building" and "landscape"; it allows for the simultaneous presence of the one within the other, buildings as landscapes, landscapes as buildings.

21. Alejandro Zaera-Polo and Farshid Moussavi
The conflict between a rational, artificial, linear geometry and a picturesque reproduction of nature through less determined geometry has structured the history of landscape. It is through overcoming this opposition that we think the possibility of an emerging landscape, and city, and architecture may exist. The emerging landscape will be characterized by developments that are already happening in biotechnology, artificial intelligence... "complex" organizations, generated through the negotiation of multiple orders: the geological, the biological, and climatic, in a morphogenetic process.

22. Robert Smithson
My dialectics of site and nonsite whirled into an indeterminate state, where solid and liquid lost themselves in each other. It was as if the mainland oscillated with waves and pulsations, and the lake remained rock still. The shore of the lake became the edge of the sun, a boiling curve, an explosion rising into a fiery prominence. Matter collapsing into the lake mirrored in the shape of a spiral. No sense wondering about classifications and categories, there were none.

23. Reyner Banham
Within its vast extent can be seen its diverse ecologies of sea-coast, plain, and hill; within that diversity can be seen the mechanisms, natural and human, that have made those ecologies support a way of life—in the dry brown hills the flood-control basins brimming with ugly yellow water, the geometries of the orange-groves and vineyards, the bustling topologies of the freeway intersections, a splatter of light reflected from a hundred domestic swimming pools, the power of zoning drawn as a three-dimensional graph by the double file of towers and slabs along Wilshire Boulevard...

LANDSCAPE

24. Jesse Reiser

Landscape admits of no single determination. It has a potential to be open enough to change over time, putting forth form and organization over program—in other words, there would be a loose-fit logic between the program you are proposing and the organization that you are developing. For instance, in Central Park, Olmsted designed zones for a general set of uses defined for him by certain nineteenth century practices—the sheep's meadow for grazing, for instance, could also accommodate people strolling in an open space. That same meadow wouldn't be understood through the picturesque today, and might even be used for rock concerts; these Olmsted could not have known about but could nevertheless be said to have allowed for. The Rambles, used in the nineteenth century by courting couples has since the early 1990s become a gay trysting spot—it is still for the interaction of people, but the practices have changed.

25. Stan Allen

Much more than a formal model, landscape is important to architecture and urbanism as a model of process. Landscapes cannot be designed and controlled to the degree that architecture can; instead, landscapes, like cities, are loosely structured frameworks that grow and change over time. Landscapes are immersive environments, diagrams only partially controlled. Time is a fundamental variable in landscape work. Even the most static, traditional landscape requires constant management in order to maintain a "steady state." Today, landscape architects are embracing change and designing landscapes that anticipate a succession of states: a choreography of changing plant regimes, shifting spatial characters, and new uses over time. These changes are not merely quantitative—plants growing into maturity—but are qualitative as well. Working with a precise spatial framework, the designer creates the conditions under which distinct, and perhaps unanticipated, spatial characteristics may emerge from the interplay between designed elements and the indeterminate unfolding life of the site.

26. Keith VanDerSys

Nature is dead.

More than a century ago, Friedrich Nietzsche proclaimed the death of the sovereign moral beacon: as the center of knowledge and meaning, who represented a shared belief system that both defined and unified a disparate collection of cultures. The demise of God is not just a negation of order but a complete rejection of any absolute value system, ending accepted standards of morality and purpose, and forcing a new mode of being derived by cultural norms rather than an absolute "other."

Pictorial modes have typically dominated landscape practice over the last five centuries. Such paradigms, biased by compositional techniques of painting and poetry, organize landscape as an aesthetic object, emphasizing appearance and narrative. This ideological conception of landscape, as a representational intermediary, constructs a view of the world around an anthropocentric object and a nonhuman periphery, a condition that both objectifies nature and problematizes it as something "outside" or "other" from cultural persuasion.

Oppositional center-periphery structures produce a form of landscape that is static, bounded, and territorially separated—a progression of identifiable types moving inward from wilderness (supposedly absent humanity) to degrees of acculturation: agricultural, rural, suburban, and urban. Such model-copy formats, built around Edenic dreams, assume nature as a once-felicitous garden habitat in a state of decline, now wanting in plenitude and futilely struggling for an unattainable return. Nature and culture are thereby locked in an irreconcilable split where "natural" things are perceived as good and "unnatural" as bad. This underwrites much of the moral authority of landscape with its unassailable appeal to nature as an external source of universalizing norms.

Edward Casey has suggested substituting "wildness" in favor of "wilderness" as the ideological compass for conceptualizing, organizing, and imparting value in landscape. "Wildness," unlike its territorialized and legible cousin "wilderness," occurs everywhere. It is shapeless and limitless, more process or moment of an environment. This transposition challenges the apparent naturalness of the signifying relationship between nature/culture polarities, shifting landscape conceptualization toward an ecological modality. As such, systems comprised of exchanges and interrelations create situations between things that are privileged over subject/object production by things. Landscape, here, is reimagined as a verb rather than a noun; it becomes a constellation of processes instead of compositional objects.

If the park is the emblematic ground of a wilderness ideology that once dominated landscape practice, then the beach is now the supreme recreational field that best characterizes its contemporary status. Beaches, unlike parks, are comprised of unstable margins and ever-changing surfaces affected by an array of provisional forces. The shapeless and ephemeral border between land and water is an elastically ambiguous threshold subject to trajectories of varying magnitude. The superlative activity of parks was strolling. Surfing, then, is an obvious mode for activating and operating in provisional landscapes. Unimpeded by plan or path, surfing acts tacitly to cruise the dynamic fluid surface, subtly effecting and reacting to the rhythmic yet radical vacillations between moments of horizontal and vertical topographic plasticity. Grab a board and jump right in. The water's fine.

LANDSCAPE

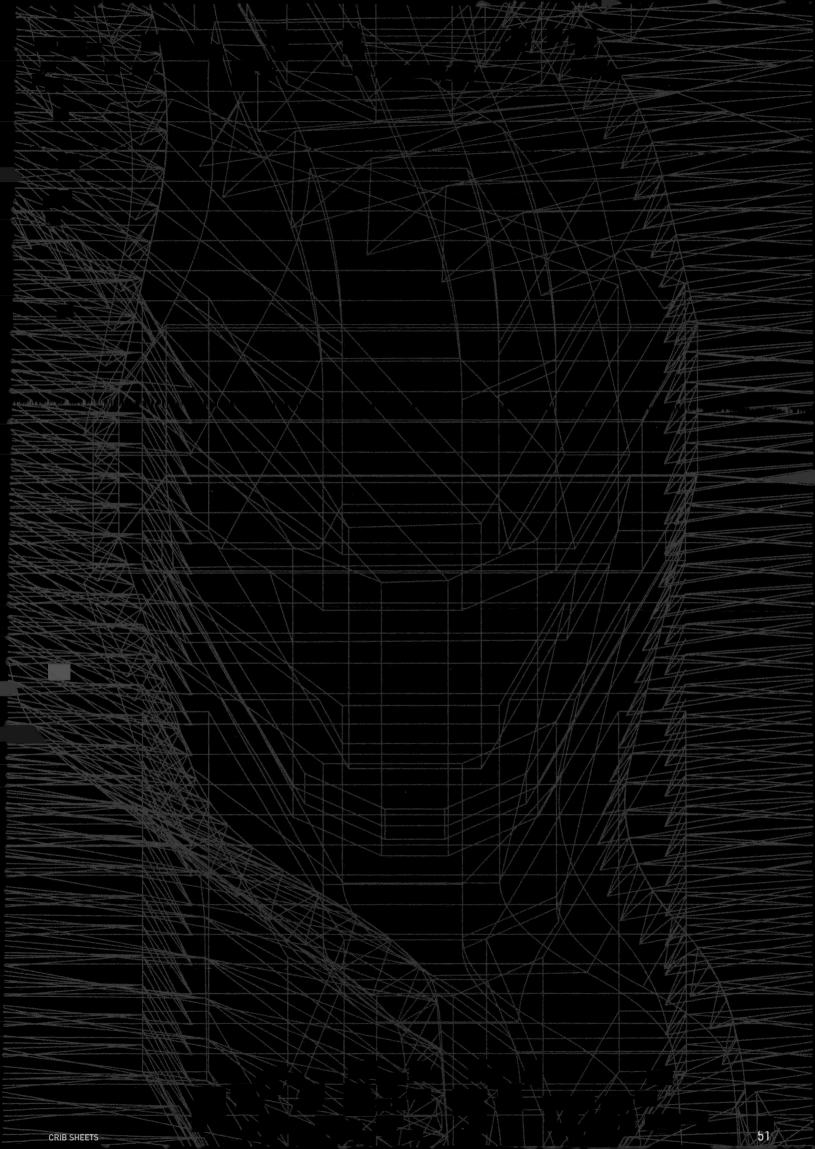

The Blur building is an experiment in de-emphasis on an environmenta scale.

ENVIRONMENT

2. Lars Lerup
Brown fumes. Fiery sunsets. Pollution fills the days when the weather rests.

3. Siegfried Kracauer
Remnants of individuals slip into the nirvana of relaxation, faces disappear behind newspapers.

4. Charles Jencks
If Hans Hollein in the 1960s declaimed *"alles ist architektur,"* where does that leave environment?

5. Mark Wigley
Architecture is to be found in the relationship between atmospheres, the play between micro-climates.

6. Seth Rubin
Disney World is the first copyrighted urban environment in history, a Forbidden City for postmodernity.

7. Robert Venturi, Denise Scott Brown, Steven Izenour
The artificially lit, air-conditioned interiors complement the glare and heat of the agoraphobic auto-scaled desert.

8. Peter Blake
Crisscrossed by highways lined with billboards, jazzed-up diners, used-car lots, drive-in movies, beflagged gas stations, and garish motels.

9. Sylvia Lavin
The house leaks amorphously beyond its physical perimeter through expansive window-walls and seeks atmospheric continuity with its environment.

10. Mark Goulthorpe
That is a real compulsion for us: exploring how to create an environment that engenders a sense of precise indeterminacy.

11. Greg Lynn
The blue video bile transformed to a warm incandescent glow. Its irritation amplified with the muffled sound emanating from its interior.

12. Philip Johnson
All architecture is shelter, all great architecture is the design of space that contains, cuddles, exalts, or stimulates the persons in that space.

13. Achim Menges
Environment is understood as a dynamic composite of habitat-specific conditions and in habitant-specific itineraries, a gradient field of performative micro- and macro-milieus.

14. Richard Neutra
Architecture is illuminated not only by light but by sound as well; in fact it is brought into relief for us through all our senses.

15. Reyner Banham
Drive down the last leg of Wilshire towards the sea, watching the fluorescence of the electric signs mingling with the cheap but invariably emotive colours of the Santa Monica sunset.

16. Michael Hensel
A design environment in which the generated is always to some extent different from the anticipated, and in which the unfamiliar appearance and behaviour of transitory states becomes the focus of interest.

17. Paul Virilio
The way one gains access to the city is no longer through a gate, an arch of triumph, but rather through an electronic audiencing system whose users are not so much inhabitants or privileged residents as they are interlocutors in permanent transit.

18. Paul Scheerbart
An increase in the intensity of light is not what we need. It is already much too strong, and can no longer be tolerated by our eyes. Tempered light is what we need. Not "More light!" but "More colored light!" must be the call.

19. Michael Bell
Environment is a useful term only in the general sense of location and the potential operative techniques an environment may offer. If understood as something to sustain— as in "the environment"—this theme will slowly but surely take over and even supercede our current practices.

20. Russell Fortmeyer
Environment is the term to which architects give a passing nod when it means the limited supply of natural resources and regions from which building materials, and in which buildings themselves, are produced. But environment is also the combination of atmosphere, geometry, and style that produces effect.

21. Brett Steele
Architecture is migrating away from the static composition of inert, dead, building materials and moving towards dynamic and interactive components and interfaces. The kinds of immersive environments created by these possibilities are able to anticipate as well as adjust themselves to emergent patterns of their own use, inhabitation, and transformation . . .

22. Servo
Within architectural and art historical legacies, an environment is that which synthesizes formal and programmatic systems, machinic processes, and atmospheric effects. The potential of the respective technologies that form these systems, processes, and effects is an interlacing, a fusion, or tectonic that situates the environment as both a method of production and communication.

23. Rem Koolhaas
Gravity has remained constant, resisted by the same arsenal since the beginning of time; but air conditioning—invisible medium, therefore unnoticed—has truly revolutionized architecture. Air conditioning has launched the endless building. If architecture separates buildings, air conditioning unites them. Air conditioning has dictated mutant regimes of organization and coexistence that leave architecture behind.

24. Helene Furján
Environment is both the context within which architectural productions occur and exist, and architecture's constitution of a setting for human actions and events. Today the term circulates in apparently contradictory ways: it is both a sociopolitical concern (including "environmentalism"), and a concern with the experiential aspects of architectural space and form (atmosphere, effect, and mood).

25. Constant
With no timetable to respect, with no fixed abode, the human being will of necessity become acquainted with a nomadic way of life in an artificial, wholly "constructed" environment. Let us call this environment New Babylon and add that it has nothing, or almost nothing, about it of a "town," in the traditional sense of the term.

26. Sulan Kolatan
Currently, we are preoccupied with operating "environmentally" in the broadest sense possible. This is a question of medium: in so far as environment denotes a "world" constructed of multiple systems bound together to create specific surround effects—real and/or perceived—the definition of architecture includes virtual and ambient media. It is also a question of generic class: architecture is inextricably linked to other natural and artificial systems of production and consumption.

27. Jean Baudrillard
You have only to see Las Vegas, sublime Las Vegas, rise in its entirety from the desert at nightfall bathed in phosphorescent lights, and return to the desert when the sun rises, after exhausting its intense, superficial energy all night long, still more intense in the first light of dawn, to understand the secret of the desert and the signs to be found there: a spellbinding discontinuity, an all-enveloping, intermittent radiation.

28. Stephen Bayley
There are people who, at home, have Great Exhibition floral carpets, purple Dralon suites, prints of Big Ben or wild animals, a music centre, DHSS lighting, the *AA Book of the Road*, stale air, ornaments, processed food, German wine, white bread, artificial fabrics, and novels by Jeffrey Archer, who enjoy, when they are on the road, the sober, controlled environment of their Nissan Cherry where colours and details have been meticulously thought out.

ENVIRONMENT

29. Marc Augé

Non-places are the real measure of our time; one that could be quantified—with the aid of a few conversions between area, volume and distance—by totalling all the air, rail and motorway routes, the mobile cabins called "means of transport" (aircraft, trains and road vehicles), the airports and railway stations, hotel chains, leisure parks, large retail outlets, and finally the complex skein of cable and wireless networks that mobilize extraterrestrial space for the purposes of a communication so peculiar that if often puts the individual only in contact only with another image of himself.

30. Jesse Reiser

The foundational ideas of our work are grounded quite literally in the flow of natural systems. The development of computational models to simulate flocking behaviors, for example, have permitted the study of systems with no organizing agent, where discrete elements work within simple rules to generate complex behaviors, and where the behavior of these systems is not reducible to the sum of the elements involved. Nevertheless, such models pale before the actual behavior of birds—or for that matter, the behavior of magnetic fields in the real world. For this reason, scientists working in the fields of material behavior utilize these reductive models only secondarily, relying upon the actual interactions of materials and experiments. In our work we look to the diagrammatic uses of these behaviors for architectural organization, related to the question of scale.

31. Marc Sanchez

From the end of the nineteenth century to the present, the term *environment* suffuses architectural discourse, from its deployments in early twentieth century modernism, through the post-Second World War pedagogy and practice of "Environmental Design," to its recently-held position in rhetorics of sustainability. In each of these differing valences, however, the "environment" that architectural discourse describes is persistently wedded to ethics, invoking an architecture that is both responsive and responsible.

The term also plays a central role in architecture's form-function paradigm, in which a "social environment" and architectural form are understood to act on one other. The concept of environment [milieu] is often traced to Aristotle, who describes it as a harmonious relationship between an organism and its surroundings. This balanced scene contrasts with the more abrasive pairing envisioned by the late-eighteenth century biologist and evolutionary theorist Jean-Baptiste Lamarck, who describes an inherently destabilizing relationship between organism and surroundings. In Lamarck's scheme, an organism's body is marked by its continual struggle to adjust to its environment; habitually repeated physical adjustments, in turn, lead to inherited traits. While this account of generational mutation would fall prey to Darwin's theory of natural selection, Lamarck's description of the relationship between an organism and its surroundings would enjoy greater longevity. It would, in short, be appropriated by architecture (via sociology) to explain the "built" environment's capacity to effect behavioral changes in people.

More recently, environment is manifested as an increasingly degraded, polluted, and perhaps sustainable entity. Reversing the Lamarckian model, a teeming humanity now consumes and increasingly surrounds the environment, which in turn must adjust to the stress of its human surroundings. Nature thus comes to surround nature, and environment, oddly, surrounds environment. Architecture's sustainable practices are conceived in this matrix of inversions and encirclements. For the most part, present discourse on environment turns away from the behavioralist and environmental determinist ambitions of research and design that proliferated in architecture in the 1960s and 1970s. Despite these disavowals, however, present accounts often retain the ameliorative ambitions that accompanied previous models. If environment cannot be cleanly extricated from these earlier efforts, how might this seemingly all-pervasive entity be redeployed to generate unforeseen effects?

Some tentative answers may be proposed. The quasi-architectural projects and experiments of mid-1970s environmental design, for example, imagined the computer as a rapidly evolving data-extracting and -visualizing instrument, one whose growing capacity and speed ultimately promised to uncover important relationships between form and effect. With the ongoing interest in digital environments, it remains to be seen how this promise has been transformed, and what aspects of environmental design's digital ambitions linger in contemporary architectural production.

Sustainable practice presently imagines that it takes part in the responsible husbandry of finite "natural resources." This external nature would presumably find its corollary in a human nature that could be managed in a similarly responsible manner. Thus we again seek to protect human nature from producing and exposing itself to harmful environments, since we (for better or worse) are susceptible to the environment's healthful, toxic, or otherwise forming forces. It is now long overdue for architecture to imagine an "environment" that is not hobbled by its connections to a universalized human nature, but which instead appears in contemporary, wholly constructed, conditions.

ENVIRONMENT

SURFACE

Eye
candy

I sacrificed volume to surface.

2. Sheila Kennedy

Electrical effects fuse with materiality; infrastructure merges with the material surface.

3. Sylvia Lavin

The surface [becomes] manifestly effective rather than tectonic when architecture seeks mood instead of meaning.

4. Alex Wall

The urban surface is dynamic and responsive; like a catalytic emulsion, the surface literally unfolds events in time.

5. Frei Otto

From a single chain, I then went to work with a net of chains, and from there I moved to the minimal surface. A minimal surface can be made very exactly with soap film.

6. Michael Hensel, Michael Weinstock, Achim Menges

The combination of the need for flexure and sufficient stiffness for stability [in tall buildings] requires the criteria of efficiency to be rethought ... [leading to] models of surface structures that exhibit the ability to flex without collapse.

7. Helene Furján

Surfaces today are increasingly activated: whether the cosmetic blurs of color, translucency, and dematerialized fogs, or the intricate geometries (deformations, castings, and inscriptions) that generate surfaces from and of themselves, surface operations are moving in the direction of hypereffects.

8. Guy Julier

The project on Disney (1995) skillfully illuminates how its public-relations machinery, its layout and detailing and the training of its staff is tightly assembled in order to maintain an unbroken surface so that the visitor may never get behind the scenes, so to speak, and experience anything of it as a producing system.

9. Ellen Lupton

Chemical peels remove the outermost layer of the epidermis, erasing sun damage and other blemishes by exposing a fresh layer of cells *skin is both dead and alive*. The thin outer layer, the epidermis, consists of strata cells that migrate toward the surface, where they compact into a layer of dead material. Skin's protective function relies on the inertness of this outer surface.

10. Johan Bettum

The problem of the architectural surface—or more precisely, the methodological development of this surface—defines the state of art-architectural practice. As opposed to all previous understanding of the surface, including the recent pre-occupation with surface topology, it necessitates both a temporal and three-dimensional conception of the liminal condition of architecture. It embodies the ongoing effort to capture the nature of events and how they produce affects.

11. Gottfried Semper

I think that the *dressing* and the *mask* are as old as human civilization and that the joy in both is identical to the joy in those things that led men to be sculptors, painters, architects, poets, musicians, dramatists—in short, artists. Every artistic creation, every artistic pleasure, presumes a certain carnival spirit, or to express it in a modern way, the haze of carnival candles is the true atmosphere of art.

12. Michael Hensel

By what means can the project of dynamic surface activation escape the legacy of object-design—the designer's finite engagement with the product—and engage instead with the open-ended, heterogeneous and temporal relation between subject and surface as a way of space-making? In what way can such an alternative approach to design acknowledge and incorporate indeterminability and contingencies relative to the way in which material surfaces might be appropriated, without merely becoming incoherent problem-solving actions?

13. Cecil Balmond

There are many proposals of free forms, or "blobs," which appear very seductive on the computer screen. Interesting as they are, there is not much point when the result is surfaces that are essentially cladding. Structure is then needed to underpin the shape, and a lot of structural work has to be done in order to make the spaces viable. This experimental work was important, and deserves respect, but it will remain a fad unless it takes on a structural integrity.

14. Paul Virilio

From the fence to the screen, by way of the rampart's stone walls, the *boundary-surface* has been continually transformed, perceptibly or imperceptibly. Its most recent transformation is perhaps that of the *interface* . . . "Every surface is an interface between two milieus in which a constant activity prevails, taking the form of an exchange between two substances placed in contact with one another." This new scientific definition illustrates how contamination is at work in the concept of *surface*: the surface-boundary becomes an osmotic membrane, a blotter.

15. Michael Bell

Jeff Winogrand's 1964 photograph of a picnic at White Sands, New Mexico, reveals a more complex surface than any of the forms depicted: it's the elastic and absent surface of an entire era that seems present here. The surfaces of the car, the picnic shelter, the sand are all complex and describable, but it is the elastic space that connects them invisibly. Hans Namuth's film of Jackson Pollock painting on glass is close to how I see this: it's the tension between something actual and its projection into space. The surface of Winogrand's photo really cannot begin to connect these artifacts—nor can the sky.

16. Neil Denari

Beyond the many possible interpretations of surface as a material or geometrical aspect of architecture lies a question of how it is coded or instilled with an idea. For instance, I have spoken of a type of coded surface called the "worldsheet." It refers to both the string theory worldsheet, a two-dimensional surface with one dimension of space and one dimension of time, and also to a more speculative cultural analysis of globalization where the "worldsheet" refers to continuous abstract development. A "surface model" of design can have possible codes inherent within it, such as "antitypology" or "territorial/expansiveness," depending upon how the geometry of the surface is used. Whether superflat, topological, faceted, illusionistic, or dematerialized, surfaces are like fly paper: they are designed to pick up codes, concepts, or performances with ease.

17. Marc Angélil and Sarah Graham

Flow-Surface: exposing form to genesis, structure to flux, a conception of architectural morphology emerges where the object's discrete boundaries seem to dissolve. The incorporation of dynamic systems within the definition of the enclosure undermines the stability of the object as a condition of rest. Fundamental to this understanding is the treatment of the object's surface as a figuration of fields. By conceptually offering a flow of perpetual motion and of continuous multiplicity, heterogeneous yet coherent architectural assemblies are suspended in a temporal dimension—endlessly searching for another, then another, and yet another form. Intrinsic is the tendency to transgress physical perimeters, or to blur contour lines, a strategy capable of serving diverging tasks. On the one hand, it aims for disjunction by weakening holistic masses; on the other hand, it aims for coherence by linking disjointed organizations into a congruous whole. The effect of indistinctiveness is pursued by way of surfaces that contain but do not define.

18. Clover Lee

It is important for architectural research to harness materials to the physical attributes of referential space. This could be achieved through decoding the "ordinary" or "conventional" building technologies, such as skin and frame or cast-in-place structures, in order to recode them into the equation of form-making process. Paying equal attention to ingenuity in construction and materiality, form-making becomes a multifaceted generative system where the virtual representation of space and the constructed reality results in an oscillating and reciprocal relationship. This decoding and recoding process, pertaining to site and surface as simultaneous generators of architectural space, extends the focus beyond form and object-making by exploring the possibilities of building systems and tectonics, which can create intelligent surfaces. The disintegration of the monolithic surface into separate layers or components allows the manipulated surface to react to influences at varies scales and magnitudes. As the surface generates form, the form-making process as an index of multivalent systems fundamentally changes.

19. Stan Allen

Landscape is, at one level, an art of surface. Landscape's traditional terrain is the extended horizontal surface; more recently, that territory has expanded to include topographic surfaces that are folded, warped, bent, or striated. This has an obvious attraction for architects today, where surface has become a primary instrument in design. However, distinct from the proliferation of thin, transparent surfaces in contemporary architectural design, landscape surfaces are always differentiated by their material and performative characteristics—or better, in landscape, performance is a direct outcome of material.

It is, in fact, slightly misleading to refer to "surface" in landscape, the matter of which is spread out in the horizontal dimension, but landscapes are never, strictly speaking, pure surfaces. The natural ecology of a meadow, field, or forest exhibits horizontal extension in the macroscale, but at the microscale it forms a dense mat: a compact and highly differentiated section. This articulated section, the "thick 2D" of the landscape, is fundamental to the work that the meadow or the forest performs: the processing of sunlight, air, or water, the enrichment and protection of the soil through the process of growth and decay. In field configurations, section is not the product of stacking (discrete layers, as in a conventional building section) but of weaving, warping, folding, oozing, interlacing, or knotting together.

Slope, porosity, hardness, soil chemistry, consistency—all these variables influence the life that a surface will support, and its own development in time. By careful attention to these surface conditions—not only configuration, but also materiality and performance—designers can activate space and produce urban effects without the weighty apparatus of traditional space-making.

20. Greg Lynn

Surface is a new word for architecture in two respects: in the way form and space are described as continuously curved sheets rather than points, lines, and planes; and in the ways that materials have qualities of color, materiality, transparency, thickness, and texture in relation to the former architecture of sheets.

Three hundred years ago, calculus provided the moment in which space and form could be described as continuous curves capable of being endlessly divided into finer and finer points. But we were cautious about losing whole numbers and even more frightened of design without our "absolute zero": architecture continued to focus on sensibilities of volumes and planes described by fixed points in space. With the advent of computer-aided-design software, it suddenly became easy to describe form and space as surfaces that can be subdivided without concern for whole numbers. We lost our fear of fractional dimensions, and surfaces became easy at last.

The sensibility of surfaces involves the invention of new approaches to fenestration, tiling, aperture, transparency, reflectivity, and mass, not to mention the simple issue of material thickness and the gradation from interior to exterior. The intractable problem of defining uniform material thickness with a calculus curve is not just a bug to be solved by software but an essential quality of working with surfaces: nonuniform thicknesses result from offsetting curves, and the difficulty gives rise to new ideas about texture, opacity, translucency, color, and pattern. For example, the ornamental reliefs, thickened bleb surfaces, and color gradients we have been developing in my office and the schools where I teach emerge from the geometric surfaces we have been designing with.

Surface is about using topology and curved-sheet geometries. Topology is capable of describing objects with flexible, transformable surfaces. In topology, there are no privileged or primary forms, such as an ideal circle, an ideal cylinder formed by the extrusion of a circle, or an ideal ellipse formed by the oblique intersection of a plane with a cylinder. There are classes of surface but not ideal solids. Surfaces are capable of describing the volume of a sphere or a cylinder, without using radius points and lines. Instead, volume is defined by the deformation of a surface through curve networks. Surface is also about the material qualities that emerge from these new shapes as they are brought into the disciplinary concerns of architecture.

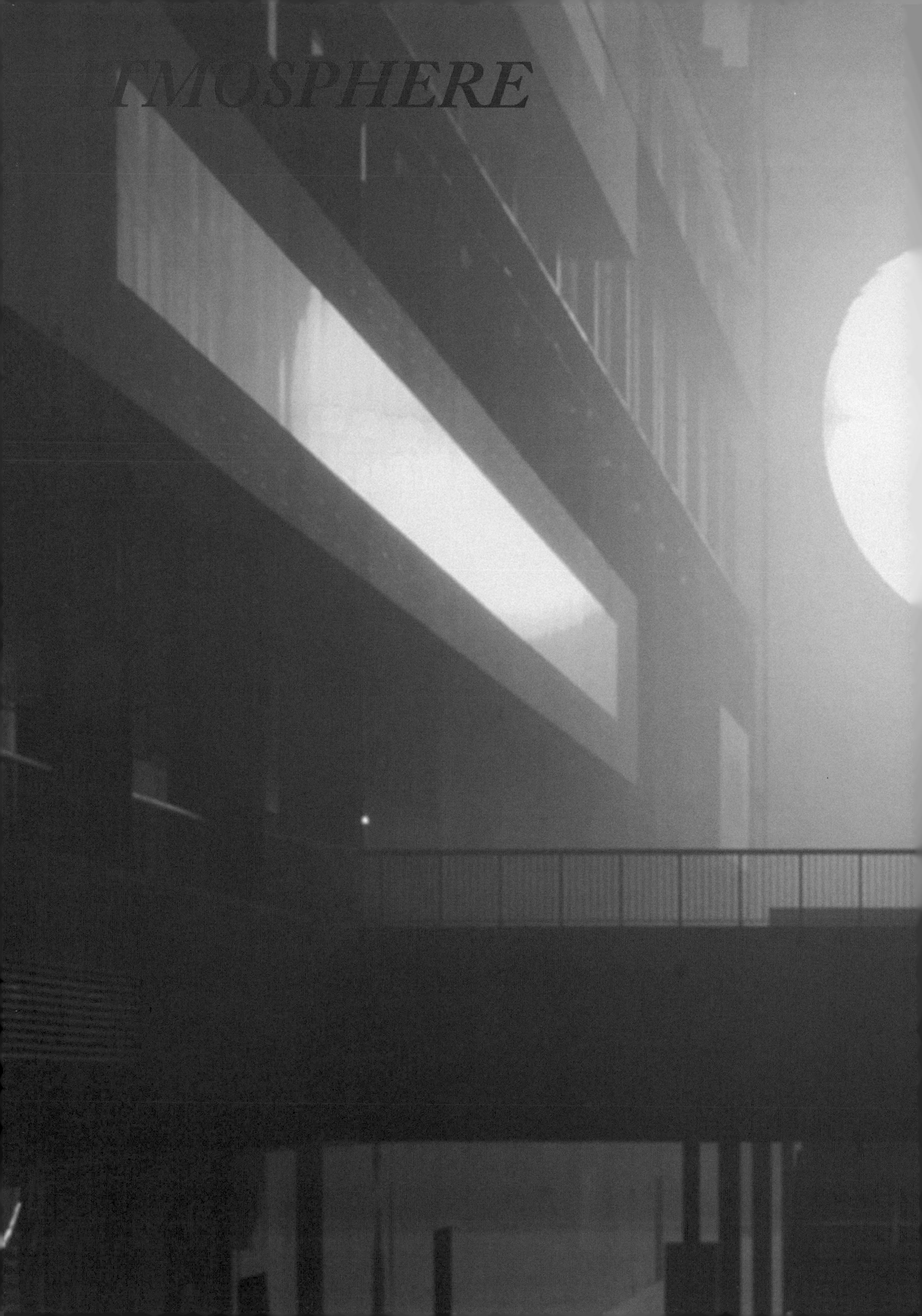
TMOSPHERE

1. Bill Clinton

I didn't inhale.

ATMOSPHERE

2. Olafur Eliasson
See yourself sensing.

3. Lars Lerup
Luminous vapors, streaks, zones, and clusters
of lights.

4. William Gibson
Hot styrene, laser printers, abandoned running-
shoes, and stale bag lunches.

5. Jeffrey Kipnis
Aesthetic pleasure, mood, and atmosphere
belong to the family of indexical effects.

6. Rachel Carson
The history of life on earth has been a history of
interaction between living things and their surroundings.

7. Gilles Deleuze
As a spectator, I experience the sensation only by
entering the painting, by reaching the unity of the
sensing and the sensed.

8. Craig Hodgetts
Atmosphere is sometimes captured but rarely
conveyed: the totality of an environment that is
more than the (architectural) sum of its parts.

9. Sebastian Weber and Kai Vöckler
By occupying and permeating a space, [atmos-
phere] creates its own zones, draws boundaries,
sets thresholds, establishes focal points, and
finally evaporates again.

10. Mark Wigley
[Atmosphere] is some kind of sensuous emission
of sound, light, heat, smell, and moisture; a
swirling climate of intangible effects generated
by a stationary object.

11. Alison and Peter Smithson
And there are, moreover, magical distortions
in which two straight-up-and-down buildings
are opposite one another. A blue glass city,
no matter how organizationally banal, is never
optically boring.

12. Dave Hickey
While The Strip always glitters with a reckless
and undeniable specificity against the darkness,
the sunset, smoldering out above the mountains,
every night and without exception, looks bogus
as hell.

13. Richard Neutra
The designed environment can and does pattern
for us many kinds of sensations which derive
from air currents, heat losses, aromatic exhala-
tions, textures, resiliences, and from the all-per-
vading pull of gravity.

14. Andy Warhol
New York restaurants now have a new thing—they
don't sell their food, they sell their atmosphere ...
They caught on that what people really care
about is changing their atmosphere for a couple
of hours.

15. John Ruskin
Our taste, thus exalted and disciplined, is dazzled
by the luster of a few rows of panes of glass;
and the first principles of architectural sublimity,
so far sought, are found all the while to have con-
sisted merely in sparkling and in space.

16. Russell Fortmeyer
Atmosphere is another way of saying mood,
the intangible aura created by the conglomeration
of sights, sounds and smells that permeate
any given architectural or landscaped space.
It is always relative to each subject and can
be highly designed, but unintended effects are
highly probable.

17. Charles Jencks
Image, *environment*, and *atmosphere* are slippery
words today, like *ambience*, *place*, *neighborhood*. As
supersegmental terms lacking clear boundaries,
and as buzzwords, they have been taken over by
the media to refer to very elastic things. Where
does the atmosphere of New York stop—in Berlin
or Bombay?

18. Servo

Architecture's interest in atmosphere is not new, but the focus in recent years has shifted from the phenomenology of atmospheres to their production through motion and technology. The best-known examples come from music videos and film, but architecture, too, can manufacture technological and ephemeral environments.

19. Constant

The ambience of an environment possessing certain specific plastic and acoustic characteristics depends on the individuals who find themselves there ... The quality of the environment and its ambience no longer depends on material factors alone, but on the manner in which they will have been perceived, appreciated and used, on the "new way of looking" at them.

20. Jean Baudrillard

In the discourse of advertising the technical need for design is always accompanied by the cultural need for atmosphere. The two structure a single practice; they are two aspects of a single *functional* system. And both mobilize the values of play and of calculation—calculation of function in the case of design, calculation of materials, form and space in the case of atmosphere.

21. Gernot Böhme

The term atmosphere is used to apprehend perceived qualities of space. As the example of stage design elucidates, atmospheres are produced through deliberate arrangements; their character, however, can be defined only by the perceiving subject. Accordingly, the aesthetics of atmospheres mediates between the aesthetics of production and that of reception ... Atmospheres are in fact characteristic manifestations of the copresence of subject and object.

22. Sylvia Lavin

Of paramount importance in the reorientation of architecture toward a field of effects de-emphasize volume, the logic of the plan, and the ethics of rationalism, in favor of atmospheres produced through the *curation* of the surface. Through accumulation, lamination, decoration, coloration, agitation, plastification, and environmentalization, these surfaces *curate* effective moods and, when these effects are special, they catalyze the contemporary.

23. Neil Denari

Once belonging strictly to the domain of thematized interior design, atmosphere has become a legitimate concern of architects where moods and emotions operate alongside ideological agendas. The need to re-invoke the human dimension of architecture without recourse to outdated modes of social concerns or body concepts plugs ergonomics and atmospherics into the programmatic matrix, cross-referenced by the colors, materials, and forms of the project.

24. Heather Roberge

More and more, contemporary culture embodies an atmosphere of flows and rhythms that are becoming overtly apparent, expressed everywhere. While highly organized as discrete entities, flows and rhythms never entirely consume their surrounding material. Always suspended within their medium, flows never resolve into disconnected bodies. The making of architecture in this context requires a method of inquiry that saturates environments with structure, which thereby produce not truthful structure but rather atmosphere.

25. Ben van Berkel and Caroline Bos

[Effects] do not operate in a pure and undiluted form, but, at best, take part in a kaleidoscope of enactments, in which the vividness of each individual effect is moderated by the simultaneous presence of other effects. Effects are actions and they emanate from relations. The best effects which architecture can produce in the contemporary world are those that are proliferating and moving, effects that are anticipatory, unexpected, climactic, cinematic, time-related, non-linear, surprising, mysterious, compelling and engaging.

26. Jason Payne

People respond viscerally to atmospheres. Increasingly they respond to institutions with ennui. We are becoming ever more a species that thrives on immediate, palpable stimulation, on material fact. It's not *what* it is so much as *how* it feels. One of the things we feel most potently in buildings is their atmosphere. Maintaining and even extending the public role of buildings demands they produce a saturated experience that almost clings to the skin of the people moving through them.

ATMOSPHERE

27. Michael Bell

From Walter Benjamin's "aura" to Jeffrey Kipnis's Mood River exhibition, themes of atmosphere are shown to exist while sustaining autonomy. Discrete things—utility objects and seductive tools—have affects beyond their apparent finitude. But atmosphere is also interesting historically when linked to chiaroscuro—and to its contemporary presence in drawings such as those of John Hejduk's Bye House. Hejduk's work, derived in part from Cubism and Purism, never relinquished a sense of literal atmosphere and, like Robert Slutzky's reading of Le Corbusier, atmosphere was understood to have presence and viscosity. Hejduk drew atmosphere: this is an amazing effect.

28. Jesse Reiser

Atmosphere and affect are aspects that the architect has traditionally maintained the agency controls. In fact, affect is a highly determined feature of architecture, whereas much of the importance ascribed to program is intractable—like sand going through your fingers. The affective dimension of architecture not only influences use; at the level of order it also describes zones of intensity that, while real, nevertheless may be experienced in widely divergent ways. Program by contrast limits these. As measure of people's practices, rather than what architecture can do, programming is a drain on freedom, on the possibility for selection, and thus on information.

29. Helene Furján

The contemporary explosion of digital media has generated a twofold erosion of Guy Debord's culture of spectacle: an "overexposure" to the flows of information and images that creates a loss of registration (a kind of digital ADD); and a shift away from spectatorship toward immersion and interaction, which breaks down the authority of the viewing subject and engages other senses—an experiential under-standing of space concerned with atmosphere and effect.

Such a sensory understanding of architecture has its links to the interest in "effect" manifested in Baroque and Enlightenment architecture, which was rediscovered by its theorists in Gothic cathedrals. From mysterious lights and moody atmospheres to the kinetics of light and shade on three-dimensional surfaces, effects were tied to temporal or climatic changes and the mobility of the spectator. Such "architectures of shadow" or sensation reached their maturity only recently, in the interactive multimedia envi-ronments of the Eameses' exhibitions, in Constant's New Babylon and its legacy in the works of Archigram and Koolhaas, or in the vibrating color-fields of Verner Panton's interiors: a flux of ludic, erotic, and strongly affective atmospheres, immersing their visitors in a psychedelic vibe (architectural "happenings"). All of these "environments"—what they are more than they are spaces—in their very deployment of multisensory effects, operate in a perceptual paradigm that resists the authorizing mode of the spectacle: distraction.

Distraction, posited by Walter Benjamin so many years ago as the mode of architectural perception, is not so much a peripheralizing inattention as it is a mood. Countering absorption, a state of observation matched to a much older visual paradigm, with a synesthetic form of perception that is optical and tactile, distractive and immersive, a distracted attention requires an active engagement with the matrix of information flowing toward the viewing subject. An organization that operates like the rapid jump cut of an MTV kind of attention, distraction is created by flooding the visual field with information, demanding, as a result, not a hyperconcentration, but an absorption that pushes perception to its limits: a distracted concentration, or a concentrated distraction. Like the diffuse fields of Diller and Scofidio's Blur building, such a perceptual mode is at once oversaturated and under-

A distracted attention is more attuned to mood than to particulars, more inclined toward the generation of feelings and emotions than semiotics. Mood and atmosphere emerge through provisional sensory effects deploying sound, light, color, and surface texture. They condition the "vibes" of animated environments—kinematic bodily immersions in fluid forms and fluid spaces. And they have made their way into retail spaces, as boutiques and department stores learn the "entertainment economy" from the entertainment industry. Mood and atmosphere script the spaces of leisure and entertainment, from club and rave venues, to bars, lounges, restaurants, spas, lobbies (especially of boutique hotels), and the immersive effects of "spectacular" shows such as those of Cirque de Soleil.

Marshall McLuhan, the first to study media in terms of effects rather than content, famously claimed that electricity was a pure medium; light, a flow of information. Today, architecture finds itself increasingly dissolved into ambient fields, relations of materials and forces in which material can flow, can become as ephemeral as light. Architecture is no longer defined through enclosure, wall, or even surface, but through surface and space conceived together, as a field or matrix of effects: immersion and surface cohere around a constellation of effects that together produce an atmospheric condition. From the aerosol properties of contemporary cosmetics to ephemeralities of light, color, and projection, properties such as hue, luminosity and obscurity lift free of the surface and diffuse into a thickened region of space, as the very matter of architecture.

Atmosphere resists the predominance of ocularity in modernism. Working either to remap vision within a bodily, fully sensory, terrain, or to obscure it, filling the air with special effects (opacities, luminosities, mists, colors) that prevent a totalizing gaze, atmospheric architecture (or architectures of atmosphere) returns the "spectator" to bodily awareness, and to a kinetic, tactile field in which they are fully immersed.

ATMOSPHERE

DECORATION

All that glitters

Less is a bore.

DECORATION

2. Roger Fry

Display is indeed the end and explanation of it all.

3. Jeffrey Kipnis

A matter of cosmetics, a hypnotic web of visual seductions.

4. Frank Gehry

The "decoration" I call it, whatever we do as architects, is usually less than ten percent of the building.

5. Rem Koolhaas

There are no walls, only partitions, shimmering membranes frequently covered in mirror or gold. Structure groans invisibly underneath decoration, or worse, has become ornamental.

6. Jennifer Bloomer

I wonder if it is possible to rescue beauty from its double binds with truth and goodness, its associations with wealth and power, its utter political incorrectness.

7. Jean Baudrillard

We are beginning to see what the new model of the home-dweller looks like: "man the interior designer" is neither owner nor mere user—rather, he is an active engineer of atmosphere.

8. Clement Greenberg

Kitsch is vicarious experience and faked sensations. Kitsch changes according to style, but remains always the same . . . Kitsch pretends to demand nothing of its consumers except their money—not even their time.

9. Mark Wigley

The body of the building and the body of the observer disappear into the sensuous excesses of decoration. To look at decoration is to be absorbed by it. Vision itself is swallowed by the sensuous surface.

10. Madonna Inn website

"Safari Land—Madonna Inn" . . . if you like Tigers, Leopards, Zebras and Elephants, you will love this room! Decor in the bathroom also carries out the bold "Safari" theme, with rock waterfall shower. Room is equipped with two king-sized beds.

11. Charles Jencks

Decoration is always contrasted with ornament, as the bad with the good. In spite of the odium, decoration is to be encouraged as long as it is symphonically organized, and tied to symbolic and architectural concerns of meaning, structure, light, and space.

12. Adolf Loos

Twenty-six years ago I maintained that the use of ornamentation on objects of practical use would disappear with the development of mankind . . . By that I did not mean what some purists have carried *ad absurdum*, namely that ornament should be systematically and consistently eliminated.

13. Walter Benjamin

To render the image of those salons where the gaze was enveloped in billowing curtains and swollen cushions, where, before the eyes of the guests, full-length mirrors disclosed church doors and settees were gondolas upon which gaslight from a vitreous globe shone down like the moon.

14. Johan Bettum

Decoration continues to pertain to both the production and critique of architecture—but only insofar as it is freed from its classical mores. As an end in itself, it has been subsumed by the problem of how to articulate the surface, whether in terms of geometry, texture or, pattern. Decoration is to surface articulation what perspiration is to the body, a sign of effort. It stems from the depths of the surface and is no superficial matter.

15. Sylvia Lavin

Theorizing the contemporary requires tools able to admit architecture's mobilization of curatorial techniques, a territory recognized neither by the modern movement itself nor by its master narrators. Domestic curation is such a tool because rather than police a divide between art and nonart, between shelter and architecture, between museum and home, it permits one to consider that staging of time. If the museum has permanent displays and the Kunsthalle temporary exhibitions, the house shows special effects, durable goods, perishables, and expiration dates.

16. Michael Bell

Parergon or Ergon? The essay by Jacques Derrida published in October in the early 1980s still resonates. Derrida's analysis of Michelangelo's *Dying Slave* questioned the role of the drapery around the neck of the figure—the clothing. In questioning what was essential and what was ornamental, Derrida made it possible to reenter the scene of meaning and to relocate the techniques of intervention. Ornament was shown to be potentially essential if not indistinguishable from ergon—and thus the stage for a critical practice was reset.

17. Craig Hodgetts

It could be argued that the impulse for decoration has been the dirty secret behind many of architecture's technical triumphs, whether it's the creation of the flying buttress that better illuminates stained-glass "spectaculars," or the virtual decor achieved by cloaking a structure in butt-glazed, low-e glass, or the most recent exercises in video walls and frits. What has changed—significantly—is the idea of content, which today must be fleeting, au courant, and enigmatic, v., let's say, ponderous, enduring, and positive, which pertained just half a century ago.

18. Greg Lynn

I have been working in my office and with students on decorative patterns that are intricately connected to the geometry and form on surfaces. By transforming the control vertices of surfaces into emitters of decorative relief, patterns emerge that are intensively linked with form, much like the patterns on an animal or plant that expand, contract, scale, and in general accentuate changes in form. Structural patterns have also been exploited for their ability to produce figurative patterns and effects akin to decoration.

19. Alice Friedman

Although often denigrated and dismissed (as being distraction or as evidence of "feminine" sensibilities) decoration in architecture frequently provides popular narratives, appealing to viewers in a language separate from, but related to, the larger-scale and more abstract language of architectural form. Decoration speaks of pleasure and of the cultural loci in which the architectural object is formed. It connects buildings to consumable things in significant and revealing ways, and—being highly gendered—it often serves as an index of gendered cultural values of particular importance to historians and critics.

20. Helene Furján

Moving beyond modernism's (apparent) repression of ornament and postmodernism's pastiche-ing of classical models of ornament, contemporary practices have developed a form of decoration that rejects the classical notion of applied ornament. No longer simply a detachable supplement, such decoration becomes constitutional, remaining inseparable form the construction of the surface, the merging of Jeff Kipnis's "cosmetics" with the surface itself. Either etched into it as imprint, or formed with, and as, the material production of that surface, the latter generating autonomous forms of decoration, contemporary decorative techniques are above all concerned with surface effects.

21. Jesse Reiser

Prominent among the dualisms that have regulated Western architectural thought has been the opposition between ornament and structure. New architectural potential arises out of a fundamental reappraisal of the status of ornament and its implications for architectural organization. Contrary to classical formulation, ornament is not subservient to structure but is in fact preeminently structure itself, while what would classically be understood as structure is an inherent subset to, and of, the general decorative organization. This collapsing of the duality has potentially far-reaching architectural consequences— though not, as one might immediately suppose, as a vehicle for producing yet another ornamentalized architecture. Rather, it uses the ornamental as a graphic instrument capable of engendering complex organizations and spatialities; in other words, those that would foster unforeseen irruptions of institutional forms and programs.

DECORATION

22. Aaron Betsky

There is an alternative history of architecture in which decoration is not just what is added onto rational construction in order to give meaning, beauty, or character to a building, but in which decoration is the essence of architecture itself. Architecture would be the gathering together of available materials into order, resulting in the amalgamation of the fleeting images produced by our consumer society through manipulation and the influence of the computer. Along the way, this material would always serve as the crystallization of the world from which it was drawn, which produced a condensed way of experiencing that world. Decoration would thus be not merely intrinsic to architecture, but would be the way in which it could be understood. The craft of appropriation would both tame the natural world and make it our own, both for the maker and the user.

23. Roger Fry

The window towards which I look is filled in its lower part by stained glass; within a highly elaborate border, designed by someone who knew the conventions of thirteenth-century glass, is a pattern of yellow and purple vine leaves with bunches of grapes, and flitting about among these many small birds. In front is a lace curtain with patterns taken from at least four centuries and as many countries. On the walls, up to a height of four feet, is a covering of lincrusta walton stamped with a complicated pattern in two colours, with sham silver medallions. Above that a moulding but an inch wide, and yet creeping throughout its whole with a degenerate descendent of a Graeco-Roman carved guilloche pattern . . . Above this is a wallpaper in which the effect of eighteenth-century satin brocade is imitated by shaded staining of the paper.

24. Alexandra Loew

In 1961 Clement Greenberg divided art into two camps: the avant-garde and the kitsch. In his seminal essay on this theme, Greenberg located the essence of art through modes of reception: high practices—difficult to read and medium specific—were distinguished from low ones—easily legible and immediately gratifying. Since Greenberg's text influenced the discipline of architecture, its autonomy is bound to these issues of difficulty and legibility. Within this discourse, decoration is conspicuously absent; shunned by the academy while thriving in lowly places like the House and Garden Network, MTV, the DIY industry, and the magazine stand.

Architecture's (alleged) expulsion of decoration has taken many tactics and is abundantly cataloged; while Loos was not the first to call for a purging, his recriminations are the loudest. Even before 1898, when "Ornament and Crime" was first published, decoration had been subject to name-calling: degenerate, debased, dirty, superfluous, dusty, feminine, primitive, and generally unworthy of gravity or consideration. Recent scholarship has uncovered these reproachful architects' "white lies," indulging in the guilty pleasures of decoration under various pretexts. Mark Wigley's formidable research on the subject elevates decoration to the status of the supplement: decoration's very presence, although covert, repressed, or disguised, indicates that architecture needs supplementation in order to be satisfied. Post Wigley, it is architecture that is embarrassed, and decoration that is not embarrassing.

Wigley's research reconciles architecture with its rhetoric, exposing the surface as a critical device for regulating modernism's ambitions. Through the coat of white paint, decoration cloaks architecture in the illusion of abstraction and undress. Ultimately, however, the surface remains decoration's only sphere of influence, and the decorative project is limited in its sites, materials, and operations. Decoration may be as thick as woven textile or as thin as ripolin, as kitsch as chintz or as cunning as cosmetics, but it is still just skin deep. But to position decoration as the practice of surface effects suggests a project that is easy to gloss over. The question today is, how might one revive and salvage decoration from its debased status?

The thermodynamics of style would be a means to theorize decoration's recuperation, and stake out some modern discipline. Whereas style in the eighteenth century required studious historical reproduction, today, style is an issue of diffusion. Subject to the laws of entropy, rather than connoisseurship or creative genius, contemporary decoration is a project of atmosphere, not pedigree. In these formulations, which have their own lineage in Deleuze and Smithson, detail-intensive and rule-laden style cools down and degrades into mood: loose, cool, and atmospheric.

While decoration's mood swings once made it easy to dismiss, today it renders architecture current, of the moment, and fashionable. Decoration combines a host of related fields, bringing together product design, industrial design, curation, exhibition, fashion, and media. It consolidates design under one roof, so to speak, and in so doing keeps architecture au courant and in step with those disciplines that move at a faster clip. While architecture grapples with its ambivalence toward autonomy, the use of decoration ranges from the carefree to the ecstatic. Rather than police its boundaries of authority, decoration languishes in an endless middle (both high art and kitsch, for example), a thick environment of duty-free pleasures. Eluding issues of legibility and difficulty, decoration diffuses high-low polarities and stages its own escape: decoration is daring, rather than dirty.

DECORATION

STYLE

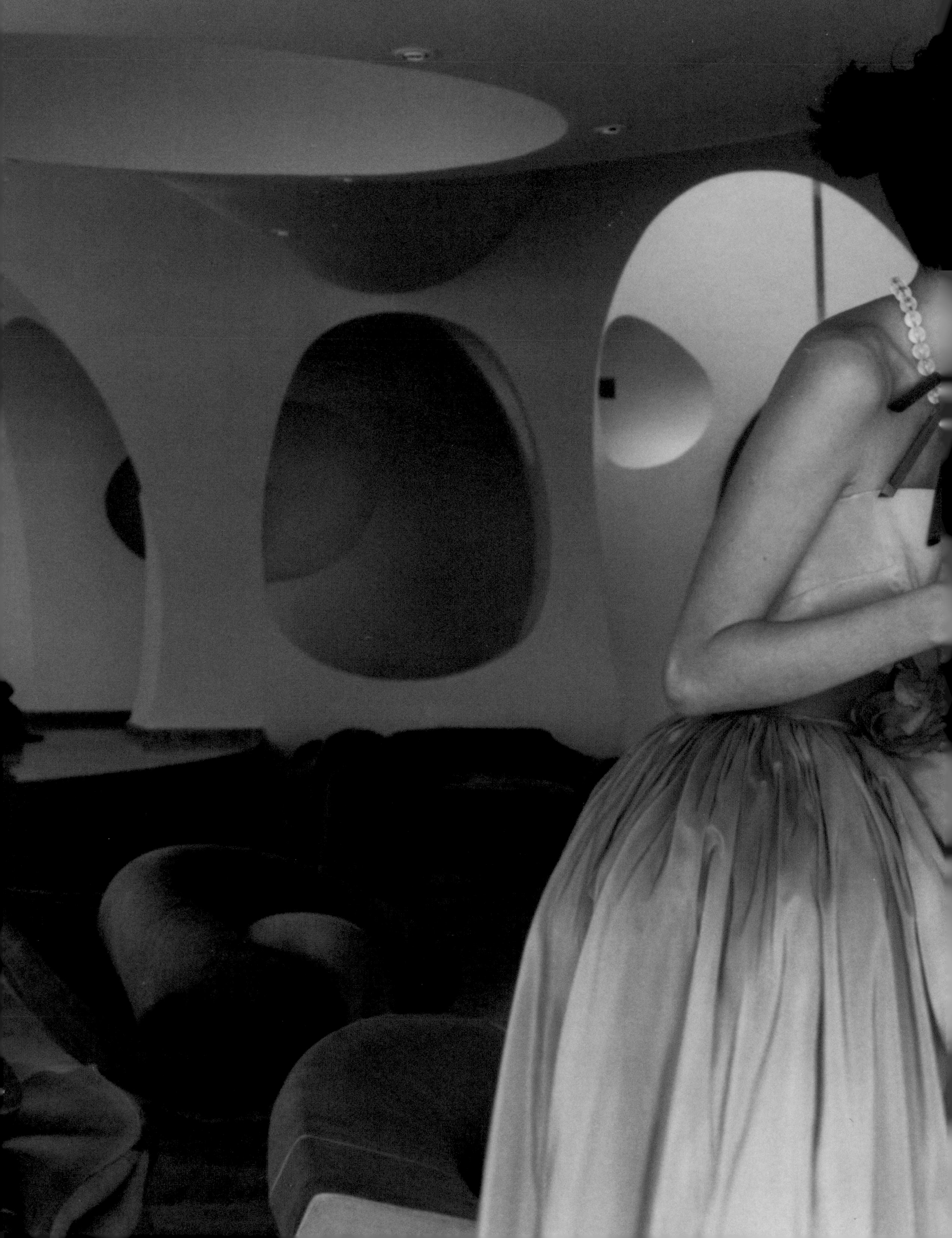

Bling bling

No space has been left unbranded.

STYLE

2. Polly Apfelbaum
Color and material could be sexy. Puddled and pink—shocking.

3. Aaron Betsky
Style is what you make it, and what makes you.

4. Ben Van Berkel and Caroline Bos
Your gaze swerves and orients you through colour, shininess, light, figuration and sensation.

5. Alejandro Zaera-Polo and Farshid Moussavi
We would not have won Yokohama if the building had not had the form of a wave.

6. R. E. Somol
Shape is illicit . . . easy . . . expendable . . . graphic . . . adaptable . . . fit . . . empty . . . arbitrary . . . intensive . . . buoyant . . . projective . . . cool . . . never having to say you're sorry.

7. Andy Warhol
Some company recently was interested in buying my "aura." They didn't want my product. They kept saying, "We want your aura."

8. Bruce Mau
I am a firm believer in what Jean-Luc Godard says: "Style is merely the outside of content, and content the inside of style."

9. Robert Venturi, Denise Scott Brown, Steven Izenour
Miami Moroccan, International Jet Set Style; Arte Moderne Hollywood Orgasmic, Organic Behind; Yamasaki Bernini cum Roman Orgiastic; Niemeyer Moorish; Moorish Tudor (Arabian Knights); Bauhaus Hawaiian.

10. Reyner Banham
A good job of body styling should come across like a good musical—no fussing after big, timeless abstract virtues, but maximum glitter and maximum impact.

11. Hugh Ferriss
A STRANGE YET MAJESTIC FORM began to loom against the New York horizon in 1922 . . . The newcomer was "uncouth," "uncivilized": it lacked "style," "scale," "taste."

12. Jürgen Habermas
The distinguishing mark of works which count as modern is "the new" which will be overcome and made obsolete through the novelty of the next style.

13. Sanford Kwinter
And the purpose of life is to bring into the world a system of novel forms that reflect the constraint of a single will or viewpoint. Style.

14. James Traub
[Donald] Trump has ascended into the Brandosphere, where an individual life becomes so immense, and so immensely desirable, that it can be marketed in the form of a purchasable lifestyle.

15. William Gibson
Google Cayce and you will find "coolhunter," and if you look closely you may see it suggested that she is a "sensitive" of some kind, a dowser in the world of global marketing.

16. Johan Bettum
Frequently shunned and derided, typically fickle and vain, style is never absent. Regardless of the qualities of a particular style, it remains the unique expression of collective sensibilities and the closest architecture comes to expressing a social engagement.

17. Michael Speaks
And it is this dynamical stability that makes an experience branded by lifestyle, which is adaptable and can change while remaining the same, more viable than one branded by identity that can only change by becoming another identity.

18. Hans Ibelings

Tourism has spawned a mind set whereby buildings, cities and landscapes are consumed in a touristic manner even when people are not on holiday, and the environment, consciously or unconsciously, is increasingly regarded as a decor for the consumption of experiences.

19. Rem Koolhaas

A Hotel *is* a plot—a cybernetic universe with its own laws generating random but fortuitous collisions between human beings who would never have met elsewhere. It offers a fertile cross section through the population, a richly textured interface between social castes, a field for the comedy of clashing manners and a neutral background of routine operations to give every incident dramatic relief.

20. Helene Furján

The demand of the "experience economy" is that experiences—and hence lifestyles—must be branded. Atmosphere and effect thus become elements of hyperdesign—special effects attached to designer signatures and coolness. The hybrid "boutique/hotel" is instructive: "boutique" is a brand-image marketing lifestyle with and as a cool contemporaneity (brand as "vibe"; "vibe" as brand), and built around hybrid programs that concentrate extreme atmospherics and extreme styling, a space of hyper-effects.

21. Roger Fry

If I were to go on to tell of the legs of the tables, of the electric-light fittings, of the chairs into the wooden seats of which some tremendous mechanical force has deeply impressed a large distorted anthemion—if I were to tell of all these things, my reader and I might both begin to realize with painful acuteness something of the horrible toil involved in all this display.

22. Bruce Sterling

Blobjects are the period objects of our time. They are the physical products that the digital revolution brought to the consumer shelf . . . Our contemporary world is absolutely littered with these things, these blobjects. Blobjects are so entirely common now that they are passé and showing their age . . . But they haven't started ruling the Earth yet. Because they're still too primitive. They're not sustainable, so they're merely optimizing the previous system.

23. Charles Jencks

If one glances through the architectural magazines of the world, one often gets the impression that there is an élite group of style-conscious popinjays whose sole desire is to provide each other with a surfeit of visual delectations. The architect's love for form, form as an end in itself, is so strong and ubiquitous that there really is an international group who follow and perform for each other and the "glossies." Yet this group is not as frivolous as it might at first appear.

24. Jason Payne

We must address the unspoken but ever-present dismissal of style as a viable contributor to architecture. For too long this has been the easiest of all criticisms to level at a body of work. Projects exhibiting "too much" style are thought to be compromised, not living up to the potentials of a purer architecture. The development of style, however, is not a reductive act but emerges in practice at the highest articulation of a coherent combination of forms and ideas. Style occurs naturally as an idiom evolves. To think of architecture as superior to other forms of cultural expression that accept, and are sometimes even driven by, style is just another kind of idealism. Style is eminently empirical.

25. Jesse Reiser

Style evolves out of practice and repetition as a way of overcoming a difficulty. Style thus emerges as a breakthrough (an innovation in technique), an overcoming of a previously intractable obstacle that then becomes available to everyone with the expertise to employ it. The repetition of style is the codification of innovation. Le Corbusier, for instance, was trying a to solve a number of problems out of which a style was innovated; the followers of this style, in deploying it for its own sake, practice a smoothed version of it. New technologies don't necessarily create new styles. All they can do is provide the conditions—the means—for innovation to occur. It is a myriad of factors in the project itself, not the individual, which determines the style.

26. Neil Denari

You either have it or you don't: this fashion axiom presents style as an innate rather than a learned human characteristic, almost like a personality trait. In many visual professions, at least those dominated by a heavy commercial force (car design, fashion, culinary arts, film, etc.), stylists exist to produce a flair, to capture the je ne sais quoi of the moment without regard for how styles actually arise or lose favor. An architect who chooses to defy the rules of style, as a means to create something new, could be seen both as either innately skilled at delivering shocking lines and bold colors or as an intellectually/politically motivated agent of disruption, whose methods won't rely on aesthetics as style but as a modus operandi of paradigmatic change.

27. Aaron Betsky

Style is both the signature of the designer and a long tradition of making that has an autonomous history but is especially responsive to changing conditions. A style can distinguish a particular epoch or period within the history of art and architecture, can serve as the signature of culture or sub-culture, class or subclass, and can enable us to discern the hand of a specific maker. We can tell the history of architecture through a succession of styles and can see their recurrence and their palimpsests as an attempt to continually restate what must and can be built in an appropriate manner. To be stylish thus means both to fit in and to distinguish one's self. It is almost impossible to define (though its attributes can be cataloged, analyzed, and typified) and thus forms the maker's equivalent of that surplus value defined from without through criticism.

28. Michael Bell

In *Japan Architect's* 1992 Shinkenchiku-Sha Residential Design Competition the jury asked for a house-with-no-style. The sole critic and the author of the competition was Rem Koolhaas, who nonetheless claimed that originality would be rewarded. I designed a house that I claimed was turned inside out as an attempt to occupy the city rather than the house, to be the city (in contrast to Mondrian's claim that the city would replace art). No style, no art. Koolhaas's call for originality was a call for the Werkbund's understanding of style: that elusive quality that allowed a work to operate as a commodity, yet retain something unknowable. Kenneth Frampton has noted that Peter Behrens worked only on the design of the objects for AEG; not how they operated. Today, we are trying to get closer to how things work, and as such, style has to be redefined to incorporate this.

29. Ari Seligmann

Style has been a persistent mechanism for categorization and distinction within architecture. Evolving out of art historical biases, the nomenclature of styles, especially period styles—Gothic, renaissance, baroque, neoclassical, modern, postmodern, etc.—endure. However, style is no longer an operative category within contemporary architectural production. This is due in part to the increasing difficulty of delineating comprehensive boundaries, because explorations in extreme form strain the links between style and language that allows style to organize meanings, and in part as a result of stylistic individuation.

Style wars and debates over "appropriate" styles drew boundaries around professional and disciplinary territories for many years. While we are no longer nagged by the question of "in what style should we build," there are still vestiges to be found in several different domains. For James Ackerman, style was a composite of conventions, materials, and techniques that transformed relationships into useful shapes for presenting historical and critical judgments, and offered classifying devices for continua of self-sufficient objects. He framed style as category.

Meyer Schapiro described style in terms of three aspects—form elements or motives, form relationships, and qualities—meanwhile equating style with language. Alois Riegl and Sigfried Giedion believed that styles were representative of the *kunstwollen* and *zeitgeist*. They helped establish style as an expression of pervasive forces.

Today it is no longer possible to maintain period or consensus styles because the proliferation of language games has atomized architectural production. Even MOMA, the preeminent style "council" that brought us the International Style, postmodernism, and deconstructivism, is stymied by unbounded diversity. Only Charles Jencks remains indefatigable, persisting in naming novelties and highlighting the current developments of his "biomorphic" and "supermodern" categories, which roughly correspond to an alternative distinction between "blobs" or "boxes." While these competing approaches exist within a continuum of formal complexity, each operates with discreet conventions, materials, and techniques that insinuate the outmoded appellation of "style."

Contemporary conventions for exploring in geometric complexity, the development of hybrid materials, and the use of innovative digital techniques exceed established architectural lexicons and challenge the simple equation of language and style. Separated from canonized associations, stylistic categorization becomes increasingly irrelevant. Meanwhile, the cultivation of personal styles and lifestyles precipitates a "styling of life"—the purpose of which, Sanford Kwinter argues, is to bring novel forms into the world. Yet these new morphologies are primarily expressions of individual determination not necessarily stylistic reflections of prevailing forces.

Going forward, we should not be confined to constructing new taxonomies, inventing new vocabularies, and fabricating relationships. We should simply abandon the need for style so as to organize architectural reception and declare Freestyle architecture. Then, as in competitive swimming, some architects may resort to crawling through the fluid discursive field, some may simply modulate their techniques to improve performance, while others will reform dynamics, propelling architecture in new directions and reconfiguring periodicity in its wake.

STYLE

This is this.

AUTONOMY

2. Hans Hollein
Everything is architecture.

3. Frank Stella
What you see is what you get.

4. Neil Denari
"The independent" (autonomy) only exists within more minor landscapes of radical difference.

5. Reyner Banham
There is nothing else with which to compare it, and thus no class into which it may be pigeon-holed.

6. Bernard Rudofksy
Space, it seems, is something valuable to us only as far as it can be bought, sold, or rented.

7. Dave Hickey
I told them that I missed "standing alone"—the whole idea that "standing alone" was an okay thing to do . . .

8. Jeffrey Kipnis
How does architecture produce irreducible effects? How does it produce effects that belong entirely to architecture and that in some sense are a version of the form of its own autonomy?

9. Mark Mack
If you think about architecture or design in too autonomous a way, you end up in a very elite position. In a more populist stance, there is more value in merging than separating.

10. Alejandro Zaera-Polo
Autonomy implies the capacity of a practice to develop such a level of consistency on an abstract level as to extend its potential effects beyond its mere efficiencies and into a regime of excess.

11. Brian Massumi
The autonomy of affect is its participation in the virtual. *Its autonomy is its openness*. Affect is autonomous to the degree to which it escapes confinement in the particular body whose vitality, or potential for interaction, it is.

12. Alejandro Zaera-Polo
Despite the fact that everybody can identify the Bilbao Guggenheim as part of the high end of architecture (it's a very expensive building), there is probably no more populist architecture today. It is possible to engage people deeply with a very speculative, avant-garde, experimental, self-referential, and autonomous piece of architecture.

13. Clover Lee
The divergent strategies of formal and operative logics in design bring into question the autonomy of the discipline. Both strategies perform within "conditioned autonomy," where the dominance or elasticity of the design is neither real nor absolute. The acceptance of this circumscribed situation allows for flexible determinacy and uncompromising indeterminacy.

14. Johan Bettum
The question of autonomy can only be posed on the basis of intense ignorance of the self's insufficiency or intellectual buoyancy and faith. Architecture embodies all of these. The autonomy of architectural practice and discourse is the retention of a bold and naive innocence—exactly what should be prescribed in times of overpowering fluxes of fashions and capital.

15. K. Michael Hays
Over and against resistance and autonomy—or better, resistance *through* autonomy—recent design theories of various stripes have tended to affirm their cultural sponsors and accept a certain determination by cultural forces outside architecture (information and entertainment technologies, in particular), over which, it is assumed, architecture has no control, and about which it has no reason to fret.

16. Craig Hodgetts

Autonomy is not in the cards. Production, supply and demand, liabilities, and the reign of empowerment conspire to channel creative effort on an architectural scale into preordained streams, each governed by strong internal consensus. Thus, over the past two decades the aesthetic/political trajectory of "meaning" in architecture has ricocheted from one establishment to another, often with no apparent rationale.

17. Tulay Atak

Autonomy is a political position. It has to do with the role architecture has claimed for itself in society, its assertion of vanguardism. It defines the boundaries of the invisible bubble within which architecture can act, and can reinvent itself. Only after this internal reinvention can architecture become an agent of external change. But is autonomy, with the space it defines for architecture, the only valid political position, or can there be less bounded positions in networklike movements? Is autonomy the only way for change now?

18. Peter Eisenman

While traditionally any project of autonomy was primarily formal, autonomy is being proposed here as a means of unmotivating the architectural sign; that is, as a means of cutting the sign off from its previous value in function and meaning. This autonomy is neither formal nor semiotic per se; rather, it opens the internal processes of architecture to their own internal possibilities ... Architecture's singularity is, in a sense, an autonomy from which there can be no copy. Instead, it generates a constant iteration of internal difference between its sign and the form of its being.

19. Jesse Reiser

Architecture itself is not a generalizing discipline, and the principles of repetition and variance have different modalities when applied to it than when applied to consumerism. The production of unique, mass-produced items for target-marketing is an abstract notion; it doesn't effect architecture. Once items enter the market, unique variation becomes meaningful only in so far as micromarkets are exploited. Therefore the effect of the variation is analogous but not the same. Only in collective repetition does variation reveal itself architecturally. The construction has to contain enough components to make the variation within it perceptible.

20. Michael Bell

Much architecture today has inadvertently become autonomous. While a generation of architects (Rafael Moneo, Aldo Rossi, Massimo Cacciari with Manfredo Tafuri, Peter Eisenman) attempted to define an autonomous design process—and an existential relation to authorship—the United States postwar city produced countless authorless buildings within an essentially autonomous set of financial procedures. The study of the "Contemporary City" in all its guises and by all its critics forces a conclusion that autonomy is to a large degree in place already. In Cacciari's description, while the city is a site of production, familial relations remain intact and territory is still drawn within these relationships. The metropolis is, however, self-sustaining and autonomous—it draws territory from within production.

21. R. E. Somol

With the critical project, with autonomy and negation, with Rowe and Tafuri, the best you can hope for is a stalemate, or confession, or perpetual ambivalence ... As a projective alternative, it is possible to unfold Banham the way others have Rowe and Tafuri, and this program is intimately linked, as Ed Mitchell has suggested, to the negotiation over "lifestyle." One aspect of this reorientation would be to recognize (and possibly profit from) architecture's erosion by surrounding design fields, the slackening of the discipline, its dissolution into graphic, landscape, product, interior, fashion, and urban "design." All design fields are in the process of becoming-one. What's becoming "out of place" is the role of disciplinarity in the communion of information technology and the virtuality of materials.

22. Charles Jencks

No individual, profession, or nation is autonomous, all are semi-autonomous; that is, related to other individuals and institutions both up and down the hierarchies. The attempts by Rossi, Eisenman, and Venturi to base an architecture on its own ontology soon led them to further seek foundations outside the discipline. One understands the motivation to ground architecture in something sui generis, to make it a serious scientific profession with theories that are refutable and propositions that follow, but all attempts meet with a paradox. The semi-autonomy of architecture is dependent on fields outside itself. That is, by definition it is a messy, hybrid, plural, elastic discipline with some internal and many external qualities. The attempts to make it more autonomous may result in high achievements, but at the same time its vitality results from outbreeding

23. Richard Weinstein

If architecture is to maintain critical distance, it is both necessary and practical to detach formal expression from "the content of the event" from the structure of appropriate feeling inherent in the use of the building and in its institutional role. Using this philosophy, buildings should no longer look like what they are, because they really ought to be something else. But it need not follow from this analysis that form be autonomous in order for the architect to be critical of certain social arrangements. In the departure of shape from what is still generally understood to be—a traditional typology—the architect can still make a critical statement that can be communicated to the widest public. This can be accomplished without limiting the exploration of new expressive and artistic strategies, and without obscuring the connection between form and meaning.

24. Greg Lynn

Without autonomy there is no expertise and, in some cases, there is a need for specific intra-architectural knowledge. Without expertise, architecture cannot extend itself outward toward cultural, economic, and political forces.

To what degree can architecture maintain some sort of critical status if its role is to communicate or to house social-cultural events? Can it have critical content, or does it instead become a service that risks being overwhelmed by the content of the event? For architecture to be critical, it has to have distance from those events in order to engage them in a way that is architectural. To make a connection between content and architecture requires an autonomous or semi-autonomous relationship between the two. Self-conscious or self-critical architecture requires distancing effects—alienating effects that make you fully aware of the architecture and require that you read and experience it in a way that is both focusing and transformative.

25. Helene Furján

One concept that has circulated within competing modernisms and their offspring most insistently is that of autonomy, particularly since the middle of the twentieth century and within the influences of both a European Marxism and Greenbergian art theory. Autonomy is not a new concept in architecture. Emil Kaufmann in the 1920s and 1930s decisively formulated architecture as an autonomous production, borrowing the concept from German art history, particularly from Alois Reigl, and "finding" it lodged within the discourses and practices of a pantheon of architects that ranged from the "revolutionary" late-eighteenth-century French architect Ledoux to Le Corbusier, theories of genre or disciplinary specificity already present in the work of Ledoux's contemporary, Quatremère de Quincy. But it is within the discourses of modernism that autonomy has been most influential, particularly in the work and writings of Manfredo Tafuri, Aldo Rossi, Colin Rowe, Peter Eisenman, and Michael Hays, all of whom have made recourse to this concept, each in differing ways, Eisenman's, for instance, are grounded not in Marxist theories of alienation but in linguistic theories of the sign. Just as there are different modernisms, there are different autonomous practices.

Autonomy in architecture today has made a swerve away from critical theory toward a visual culture dispersed by and into the flows of digital space: the media technologies threatening to submerge architecture in their effects are met by an architectural reinvestment in the notion of autonomy. A turn to autonomy has always established a disciplinary distance from contemporary culture, but today's distancing effect is no longer achieved through architecture's own alienation—as a resistant critical practice—and no longer automatically adopts a late-Marxist lament over the (degraded) world of consumer culture, information flows, and entertainment effects. In today's disciplinary milieu, autonomy is coupled with a resistance to the very notion of criticality itself. Autonomy is rather a way to oppose a particular kind of immersion, that of negotiation—an immersion in extradisciplinary concerns that risks relegating architecture's role to that of a service.

The delineation of a particularized domain for architectural practice is also a means to carving out a terrain of operation: if architecture appropriates techniques and technologies from other disciplines or industries, how is it able to compete with those industries except by inscribing a terrain in which it is architecture's exploration of them, for architecture, that counts? Beyond merely establishing a discursive specificity, autonomy—and its link to new morphologies—becomes a means of freeing contemporary practice from its own history: typology, as precedent, gives way to the generative diagram and the generic, while the "self-similar-unique" prototype frees the architectural object from the copy, especially within mass production. The demarcation of new practices—new "signatures"—becomes a means of staking out an autonomous individual production and hence both a "market niche" and a disciplinary stake framed insistently from within the terms of its specificity. However, such "autonomy" is not that of the earlier models; it is instead a means by which architects delineate and negotiate the shifting borders of disciplinarity and expertise, not restricting architecture to an infinitesimal interiority, nor a radical exteriorization (the erasing of disciplinary boundaries altogether), but offering expertise.

Apologists of autonomy see its possibilities of resistance and criticality eroded today by the merging of architecture with the flows of electronics. In the critical approach to architecture that characterized the 1970s, autonomy provided a means to resist the collapsing of architecture into other discourses, to remain different yet related to other media in order to critically intervene in those media. Today the dissolution of architecture into the contemporary world is simultaneously accompanied by a return to its very specificity. The merging of architecture with "design" more generally—with the virtual, or with information flows and technologies—is being embraced, but it is neither as euphoric nor as totalized as might have been expected. Operating through the modality of feedback, architecture has been able to celebrate its diffusion—perhaps the end of disciplinarity as such—while at the very same time holding on to what belongs—in its singularity—its own territory.

AUTONOMY

An extremely static space then begins to move and change into a fluid space.

FLOW

2. Le Corbusier
Let us not lose sight of our aim: To harmonize the *flow* of the world's products

3. Mark C. Taylor
Stability, security, and equilibrium, however, can be deceptive, for they are but momentary eddies in an endlessly complex and turbulent flux.

4. Rem Koolhaas
Continuity is the essence of Junkspace; it exploits any invention that enables expansion, deploys the infrastructure of seamlessness: escalator, air conditioning, sprinkler, fire shutter, hot-air curtain.

5. Srdjan Jovanovic Weiss and Sze Tsung Leong
The escalator accommodates and combines any flow, efficiently creates fluid transitions between one level and another, and even blurs the distinction between separate levels and individual spaces.

6. Saskia Sassen
One of the important changes over the last twenty years has been the increase in the mobility of capital at both national and especially the transnational level.

7. Russell Fortmeyer
Flow: a cyberage term evoking the flow of information in the form of light and energy through wires and fiber connecting anyone with a computer and a telephone throughout the world.

8. John Thackara
As we move from a project model to a continuous model of design—which is increasingly the norm in information technology and in management consulting—we need new metaphors for what we do.

9. Sanford Kwinter
But to what matrix does a school pay homage? Out of which continuum does the organized twitching, the plastic geometries of the piscine field emerge? To that transparent, infinitely mysterious field of vectors, that marvel among things, to Water.

10. Fredric Jameson
The elevator lifts you to one of those revolving cocktail lounges in which, seated, you are again passively rotated about and offered a contemplative spectacle of the city itself, now transformed into its own images by the glass windows through which you view it.

11. Manuel Castells
Our society is constructed around flows: flows of capital, flows of information, flows of technology, flows of organizational interaction, flows of images, sounds, and symbols . . . there is a new spatial form characteristic of social practices that dominate and shape the network society: the space of flows.

12. Jeffrey Kipnis
The unfathomable flows that coalesce into each work of art, each work of design, each person, indeed, into each and every thing that exists: flows momentous and minute, flows of matter and organization, of knowledge, technique, and technology, of money, sociology, and politics, and ultimately, flows of desire.

13. Alex Wall
Familiar urban typologies of *square*, *park*, *district*, and so on are of less use or significance than are the infrastructures, network flows, ambiguous spaces, and other polymorphous conditions that constitute the contemporary metropolis. Unlike the treelike, hierarchical structures of traditional cities, the contemporary metropolis functions more like a spreading rhizome, dispersed and diffuse.

14. Ole Bouman
The status quo is cold, immobile and solid but Flow is hot, mobile and adventurous. And, where it's hot, things tend to happen . . . Movement is not necessary for life, movement *is* life. It is the journey, not the destination. Flow *is* no longer an expression of words, of coming and going, but a state of Being.

15. Steven Johnson

Now zoom in another level, to the individual bits of information that convey our virtual city-building to our networked compatriots. These too find their way across the infosphere by drawing on the distributed logic of swarm behavior, building their complex itineraries from below. The network is smart, but its intelligence is the intelligence of an ant colony, not a centralized state.

16. Stan Allen

Crowds and swarms operate at the edge of control. Aside from the suggestive formal possibilities, with these two examples architecture could profitably shift its attention from its traditional top-down forms of control and begin to investigate the possibilities of a more fluid, bottom-up approach. Field conditions offers a tentative opening in architecture to address the dynamics of use, behavior of crowds, and the complex geometries of masses in motion.

17. Luciana Parisi and Tiziana Terranova

Postindustrial capital . . . is held together by the circulation of decoded flows (flows of money, flows of culture, flows of people) . . . The, according to Gilles Deleuze, dissolution of the solid walls of the disciplinary society . . . has not dismantled disciplinary power so much as released it throughout the social field. Post-disciplinary power operates in a space of flows, a liquid, turbulent space which it rules by way of modulation and optimisation.

18. Jesse Reiser

Infrastructure is inherently connected to flow and quantity. It is not architectural inventions per se but material facts able to be tapped into and reworked—the question is not imagining a flow's activity and force, but rather what to do with it and how to direct it. Architecture, although physically static, enters into these conditions through organization. We contend that quantitative material organization is generative of these experiences, but not the other way around.

19. Johan Bettum

The idea of "flow," as inscribed in the phenomenon of the dynamic, remains the only feasible way architecture can return to the problem of time. But, while seemingly allied to the temporal in an obvious way, there is still no sensible architectural means of addressing flow, and it may even lie beyond the grasp of architecture. Although flow is "always already" inscribed in architecture, we may nonetheless not be in an intellectual or practical position to fully access it.

20. Michael Bell

Flows are often disrupted; movement is usually thwarted. In the United States one finds elaborate and sophisticated modes of movement and flow—banking, production, and media—but also tremendous expanses of stillness and exile. If the term *flow* is to be as useful as it is ubiquitous today, it would be in the schism between these realms. What flows and what does not could reveal the spatial properties of an American terrain vague: the systems that flow have kept many constituents stilled, threatening a malaise—an alienation—that fails to be affected by the flows of power.

21. Greg Lynn

Along with the advent of calculus-based geometries has come animation. Calculus is often called the mathematics of motion pictures, as any precise dimension must be determined by freezing an equation provisionally. Most of the digital design tools used by architects have the capacity to calculate curves without actual points, whose shapes are determined by the flow through *fixed* points, often called stream curves, and, in addition, allow for the key framing of elements in a time-based environment. For today's designers, flow is available both in curves and other elements that are the geometric vocabulary of calculus, and in the ability to animate these elements in a nonstatic medium.

22. Marc Angélil and Sarah Graham

Flow-geometry: the convention of architecture as object governed by figure-ground relationships has been challenged by contemporary investigations of architecture as a field. Fields revoke the distinction between figure and ground, dismantling and decentering the idea of the object as a bounded entity. Objects, conceptually exposed to conditions of flow, dissolve into a network of relationships. Linkages and connections delineate alliances of varying intensities, suggesting loose systems of geometry from which assemblies evolve. No claim is made for stable entities or for reduction to simple elements. Form takes the role of a provisional marker of a momentary and circumstantial condition. Appropriating traits of genetic processes, formal structures are deployed as a possibility within a field alluding to other possibilities. Architecture involves the *un*framing, or *de*framing, of the very forms produced.

FLOW

23. Neil Denari

Flow: has there ever been a word more hopeful, lush, or appropriate to the fluid and formal metaphoric qualities in architectural thought and design? The word has special appeal for any architect working in the upper echelons of cultural production—it has been a workhorse term, supplying the biological, hydraulic, and programmatic models (among many others) with a central form and concept. *Flow* could be termed a mirage idea, playing on our inclination to form it with the virtuality of its numerous implications. *Flow* is the "zelig" term for architecture: it can become anything in any given context, becoming formed by what's around it, always relying on its ability to range from conviviality to aggressiveness. Flow always works and, like concrete, steel, and glass, it is one of the great building materials.

24. George Rand

Flow refers in general to liquids and the movement of weather and water. "Fields of flow" can also be related to circuits or other means of regulating energy, as in the circulation of fluids in the body, the nervous system, transportation networks, money markets, communication grids, and so on. In human terms, flow involves circuits of desire: the underlying awareness we have of the pneumatics of air in breathing, the hydrodynamics of expended spit, of semen and blood, or the performative aspects of sound and speech. Embodied performances, such as those involving flow via the mouth, are invariably personal, libidinal, and sensual in character. The parallel in architecture is the manner in which evidence of the wandering mind and the meandering hand of the designer flow upward into the geometrical order. Built objects that display the results of these unconstrained flows have what Deleuze refers to as an "anorganic vitalism."

25. Servo

It could be suggested that *flow* became one of the primary sites for architectural design in the first half of the twentieth century. The complexities of managing transportation technologies—such as planes, trains, and automobiles—were met with optimism. While in previous centuries, architects' participation in the creation of cities had been in the construction of walls to harbor and safeguard the wealth of a nation, early twentieth-century architects embarked on the emerging project of designing spaces for exchange. Sites where multiple technologies and networks crossed over—terminals, ports, and hubs fabricated from the material of transportation technology—became territory for design.

While materials could not yet transform themselves, they could be inserted into dynamic systems. Form was a means of responding to invisible organizational systems that were structured by the computational parametrics of transport technologies. Steel and glass, for instance, could be looked at less in terms of a fascination with materiality and more in terms of their global deployment—through standardization, transportability, and reproducibility—in a network of flows that constituted the system of construction. What motivated architects to work on these sites was a fascination with integration and a belief that architectural design would play a major role in organizing what otherwise remained separated flow systems. Drawing on the great nineteenth-century engineering achievements—the Crystal Palace being the foremost example—Antonio Sant'Elia, for instance, envisioned a city of networks and layered systems no longer confined to the terminal or service hub but distributed over—and as—the urban terrain, while Jean Prouvé explored the integration of building systems and their standardized deployment.

In Heracletian terms, flow and its relation to architecture have been constructed through the temporal, or fourth, dimension. Where architecture had previously been understood as permanent, static, and a receptive of flow, post-Bergsonian time and material are no longer separate continuums but are instead bound up in one space-time-matter condition. Architecture, now the conductor of flows and itself a dynamic entity, enables and materializes change rather than constructing monuments of permanence. The city becomes, as Alex Wall describes it, an "urban surface" where the act of design lies in managing the features that situate the flows of money, information, goods, vehicles, people, services, and so on, that cross it.

Today, materials are themselves dynamic and have become increasingly inseparable from the systems in which they are embedded. Two significant transformations have occurred, expanding the relationship of flow to architectural design. First, the technologies through which the flow of information and the exchange of goods has grown smaller, at the same time, the network of flows has multiplied, allowing information to move across and through the surfaces of materials. The potential to use sensory technology, lighting, sound, and polymers to infuse material and transform their state is critical to this new embedding of flow; exchange has become more layered as wireless and sensory technologies (among others) no longer limit flow as a design principal to large infrastructures but permit its operation within the boundaries of materials, at a smaller programmable scale. Matter absorbs and sorts input and output; it is active, no longer a passive conduit of flows across or through it. Second, the phase shifts of material dynamic modulations (materiality shift, for instance, between solidity and fluidity) can be conceived in terms of computational production and its spatial choreography. And third, our ability to visualize, fabricate, and experiment with flow systems has increased, an ability enabled by numerically controlled visualization and manufacturing processes paired with interactive tools. No longer the traditional singular creator or author, the designer is instead in the position of overseeing the formation of architecture.

Exchanging information from within, without, and through enables the scale of flow to become more dynamic in the discipline of architecture, no longer relegating it to the scale of the previous century's transportation machinery. Systems and their performance are not invisible but actualized through the organization of materials that embed experience and activity. The analytical and design tools that are used to fabricate these intelligent environments are potential enablers for practice: using systems to act on the formation of practice and redistribute its flow is only possible once design is understood as a diversified and distributed system itself. If the position of the designer has shifted to that of regulating formation, a place for collaboration and a more liberal exchange of information in the design process becomes viable, collaborators inducing flow from differing vantage points of expertise. Flow, as a formative multi-authored design practice, will become an integral component of material and organization in the space of the next century.

FLOW

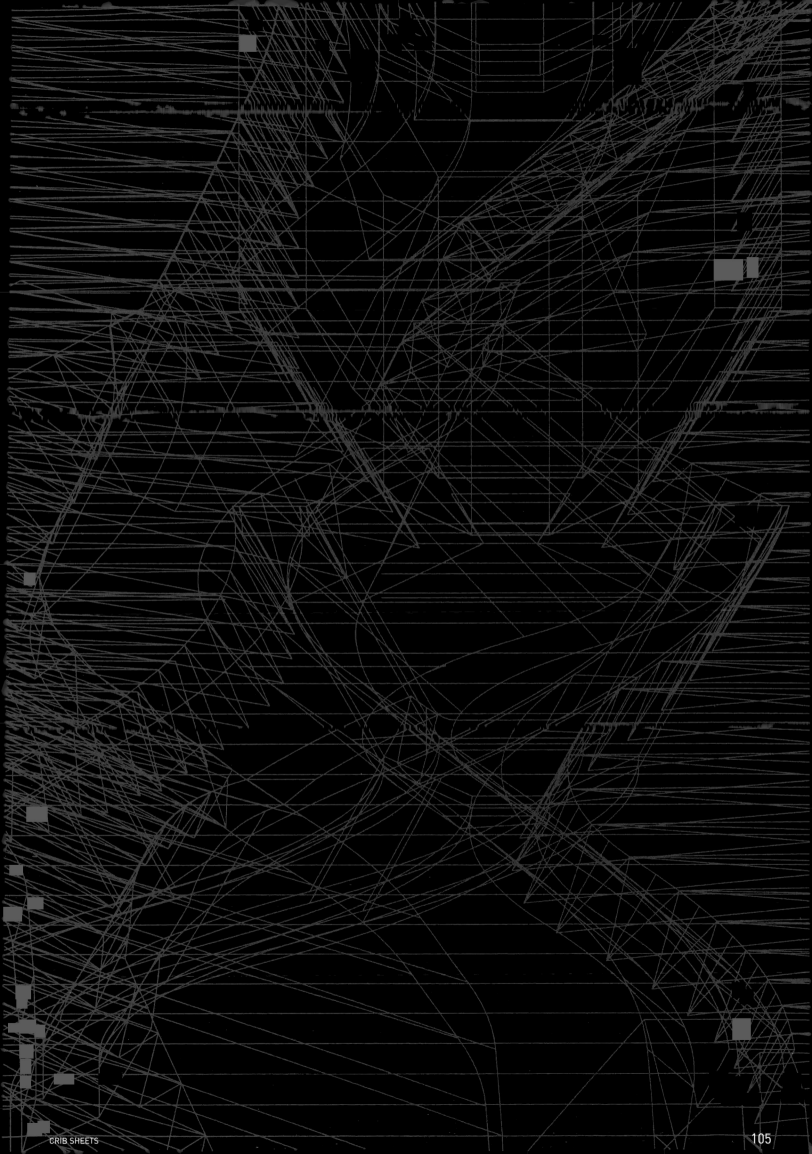

THE GENERIC

What came first, the box or the egg?

Design is everywhere, and everywhere is now designed.

THE GENERIC

2. Mark Lee

I understand the generic and the diagram as alternative iterations of typology.

3. FOA

The generic is the lowest register of singularity amongst a broad sample of cases.

4. Marc Augé

It is in the manner of immense parentheses that nonplaces daily receive increasing numbers of individuals.

5. Manuel Castells

The image of a homogeneous, endless suburban/ex-urban sprawl as the city of the future is belied even by its unwilling model, Los Angeles.

6. Neil Denari

Is the generic all good things compressed into basic formal and programmatic identities or is it completely average, a type of fundamental from which one moves toward more precise configurations?

7. Hans Ibelings

All over the world, supermarkets, shopping malls, hotels and airports have adopted a similar, recognizable form, acquiring an element of familiarity in their tacit uniformity ... These non-places can be seen as typical expressions of the age of globalization

8. Hal Foster

When the aesthetic and the utilitarian are not only conflated but all but subsumed in the commercial, and everything—not only architectural projects and art exhibitions but everything from jeans to genes—seems to be regarded as so much *design*.

9. Michael Speaks

Like Los Angeles freeway traffic, or real ants, the Generic City exhibits behavior that is infinitely more complex than the combined intelligence of all the urban savants and their instruments of control. The Generic City is on planning autopilot. Self-organizing, it absorbs as meaningless any form of intervention that seeks to give it stability, substance, layers, or identity.

10. Rem Koolhaas

The Generic City is the city liberated from the captivity of center, from the straitjacket of identity. The Generic City breaks with this destructive cycle of dependency: it is nothing but a reflection of present need and present ability. It is the city without history. It is big enough for everybody. It is easy. It does not need maintenance.

11. Helene Furján

Modernity is characterized by the genericized, privatized, neutralized enclaves generated to accommodate flows of people and capital: mutations of shopping, infrastructure, and experience into formless enclaves of simulation, and spaces of suspension—the depersonalized, homogenous hubs that demarcate the contemporary world.

12. Guy Debord

The dictatorship of the automobile, the pilot product of the first stage of commodity abundance, has left its mark on the landscape in the dominance of freeways that bypass the old urban centers and promote an ever greater dispersal. Meanwhile, instants of incomplete reorganization of the urban fabric briefly crystallize around the "distribution factories"—giant shopping centers created *ex nihilo* and surrounded by acres of parking space.

13. Dana Cuff

Both Bob Somol's house and Greg Lynn's interest in the Ford Taurus demonstrate a kind elevation of the ordinary, or a taking of the ordinary as the object or the starting point, but with each coming from totally different positions. Bob wants to see his house from a Datsun truck, while the ordinary that the Ford Taurus represents stems from an extremely sophisticated kind of technology that produces the generic.

14. Johan Bettum

While the generic recently referred to the universal and modular standardized building systems of modernity, today it represents an unfathomable realm of possibilities at once elusive and uncontrollable. The generic is the gate to the infinite expanse of the virtual; uncoded geometrical constructs are the only manner in which we can address it. Today, however, physical form continues to mask the potency of that which precedes its manifestation: the generic.

15. Michael Bell

Generic drugs, generic houses, and generic hotel rooms all have one thing in common: they question the role of the brand and offer a tempered relief in its absence. The trademark and the brand operate to supercede momentary as well as long-term changes in the organization of the object as a commodity, taking it out of time. The generic is almost a brand in itself today, removing the object from the normal commodity chain (the Muji chain, for example).

16. Steven Miles

Design, like consumption, is ubiquitous. Everywhere we turn as consumers, the impact of design is evident: from the design of a grandiose set at a party political conference or convention to the design of "corporate" university logos . . . consumer capitalism actively creates the illusion that there are differentiations in design between products. The differences in design between alternative types of jeans, between makes of jeans and types of jeans made by a single manufacturer, are often quite minor in nature and are arguably more the product of advertising and marketing than design itself.

17. Sulan Kolatan

Contemporary culture encourages the formation of chimerical classes in many different contexts, with regard to both the generic and specific. This sort of organic hybridity in which initially independent identities merge to create new classes is one of the defining productions of late-twentieth-century culture, due to the structure-generating processes of network techno-logic coupled with bio-logic. While the chimera attains its hybridity through the effects of network logic—in the de-aggregation and re-aggregation of previously sedimented institutional hierarchies, programmatic entities and so-called types—it acquires its organicity through the effects of the bio-logic, which enable these reaggregations to operate as polyvalent but unified systems.

18. Greg Lynn

The term *generic*, as I use it, refers to the not-yet-designed rather than the ordinary or everyday, the average or the familiar. It is not the ubiquitous, the chronically or terminally featureless. More in the spirit of the life sciences, it is the yet-to-be-specified, the yet-to-be-developed or differentiated. It is the shared beginning, the egg or seed, the primitive, the nonadult form. Anything that has yet to receive its final form and identity is generic (raw materials, a surfboard blank yet to be finally shaped); something finished cannot be generic by definition. The unspectacular, benign, indistinct, nondescript aspects of our world do not have the intellectual patina of the "generic." Terms used to elevate environments without merit or quality by distinguishing them from the merely mediocre, kitsch, expedient, not designed, or even badly designed are what they purport to be and nothing more: unremarkable.

19. Jesse Reiser

Both architecture and the arts are necessarily limited by their respective media, and it is precisely this limitation that facilitates their respective developments and exchanges. It would be a mistake, therefore, to overly fix on an architecture based upon the extrapolation of current trends in technology. This, however, does not mean that architecture should be yet another neutral "flexible" scaffolding that, by attempting to be good for everything, is good for nothing. This leads into an investigation into new modalities of the generic—beyond the almost universal embrace of modernism. We explore the production of spaces that are heterogeneous yet coherent. Our project for the Flux Room is a form of universal space, which deals with matter-force relations; the space of ubiquitous difference rather than the idealizing spaces of classicism or modernism. The elements of this space are simple and repetitive, yet they have a behavior and an arrangement that make them distinct from prior modernist attempts at universality. The Flux Room generates difference in the ways the space between elements is modulated rather than through the way any one element is shaped. It is an anticollage space.

THE GENERIC

20. Mark Mack

Is the generic without character, or is there character in the generic? In the past we looked at the generic as something without character and without quality. As customization and "the unique" dominate our culture, the familiar, the multiple, and the mass-produced have become seen as symbols of a social, even socialist, agenda. Does this absence of expression in our culture, at least in part, produce a less acceptable environment? While minimalism can be viewed as design's solution to this problem, the antidote to expressionist values, its intentions remain mired in the individual and the exceptional within art, and, on the contrary, do not convey the generic as a vehicle for equality and betterment. But there is a more positive definition of the generic, when looked at as a social value: as a basic element of the accoutrements necessary to form a balanced and satisfying environment.

The generic as background to the unique is a necessary element in any built environment. The Guggenheim in Bilbao, set against the gritty backdrop of an industrial and monochromatic cultural landscape, benefits from this contrast. The shopping center in the middle of a suburban sprawl distinguishes itself with a moat for parking and the large signage of chain stores. Are these two examples equal, or do we need to distinguish them by inserting value or substance? Is the generic in itself a place of value, or does it reside only in the contrast with the distinct?

What are the generic conditions in our time and in our environment? Los Angeles, perhaps more than any North American city, has a generic backbone seen in the countless single-family houses forming neighborhoods and areas of geographical distinction. The boulevards and freeways connecting these form a free-flowing, arterial live-form, supplying the generic with the blood to flow. The unique places within that form have only to be connected to these veins of transportation in order to flourish: signature buildings like Gehry's Walt Disney Concert Hall or destinations like Disneyland are successful because of the use of the generic, networked urban field that is Los Angeles. The generic single lot or home, on the other hand, could be anywhere along these lines. In this condition, the generic and the unique do not exist through mutual distinction; they simply exist. More recently, the generic has become a facade for the unique, the latter beginning to occupy the former: this development can be seen in the downtown loft spaces, the industrial warehouses of Adams Boulevard and Culver City as the new frontier in Los Angeles.

The generic holds significance for architecture not as a result of uncontrolled forces—a glorification of the unplanned, the laissez-faire—but as a conscious attempt to make architecture of value within the terrain of the everyday. The intention of the generic holds meaning beyond the self, offering a more conscious return to the appearance of more social and empathetic architectural values. It offers a more democratic overlay in a time of heightened profit values and declining social obligations barely met by cash-strapped governing bodies. From the fabrication of consciously generic housing types as a metaphor for equality, to the apparent collusion of contemporary values in forming popular taste, the generic upholds the tradition of architecture as a social construct.

22. Alejandro Zaera-Polo

Our practice has concerned itself with the exploration of typological conditions as fields of emergence, in contrast to the common understanding of typology as an entity loaded with historical significance and verification. For us, typologies are material assemblages loaded with generic solutions, already charged with a disciplinary content, and belonging to a history of architecture. We are concerned with exploring these conditions as fields of research, trying to make something generic out of the specificity of the project—but through a breakdown of typological operations rather than the proposal of such a paradigm. Typological assemblages constitute an ideal articulation of the history of the discipline, assemblages of a material, of a programmatic, social, or political nature connecting the factual environment where architecture must perform with a necessary disciplinary autonomy to grant its validity.

It is probably more appropriate to call this operation *prototypical* rather than *typological*. Both the type and the prototype operate in similar ways, but a prototype is not bound to a particular field, and does not claim, a priori, any condition of pertinence or validity. A prototype can be deployed in alternative conditions rather than remaining exclusive to a project or to a site. It is essentially an experimental tool that does not develop from existing material complexes to a particular location, but on the contrary, always tests an external organization in relation to a particular situation. Prototypes are technical and material mediators: they "mediate" information into form; they constitute responsive devices for internal and external transferral of information. As such, the prototype contains in itself the potential to absorb interference, the capacity to adjust to local contexts, and the potential to embody as much as it is to virtualize and export information into other material composites, other sites, other conditions, and other projects. In a prototypical operation, real localized data perform as an index of specific opportunities, while external models of organization operate as manifestations of different degrees of analogous global processes. A prototype does not operate in closed domains, but incorporates the notion that organizations are virtually generic and yet specific in their actualization.

A project develops from a prototype according to an operative frame, recognized and constituted as a principle, rather than literally derived from local data. That principle becomes the material mediation and the core of the organization of data. Specific technical and functional constraints may be imported and applied to infuse prototypical raw material with potential. This is the difference between a prototypical operation and emergent generation from the bottom-up (if this latter is possible at all within an architectural process): data is not the origin of organization, the core of the material, but the vector of differentiation of the prototype. Specific processes and performances are diagrammed according to the requirements of the material activation and organization of the prototype. Models for internal differentiation, responsiveness, and proliferation constitute the core, relevance, and interest of the prototype.

A prototype has an "associated fabric," and develops from a diagram that processes specific information into an architectural organization. This "associated fabric" is the result of the proliferation and differentiation of the prototype across the space of the project, reacting to the different conditions. A prototypical approach is most effective when a practice is forced to operate in many different conditions, becoming the vehicle that links different projects.

THE GENERIC

1. Ed W. Soja

City-full non-city-ness

URBANITY

2. Peter Blake
The massive, monotonous ugliness of most of
our Suburbia.

3. Manuel Castells
The global city is not a place, but a process.

4. Lars Lerup
The city's like a giant switchboard, its million
points either on or off.

5. Frank Lloyd Wright
New York: Prison towers and modern posters
for soap and whiskey. Pittsburgh: Abandon it.

6. Dolores Hayden
Asphalt Nation, Ball Park, Big Box, Boomburb,
Car Glut, Category-Killer, Clustered World,
Drive-Through.

7. Le Corbusier
A hundred times have I thought New York is
a catastrophe and fifty times: It is a beautiful
catastrophe.

8. Steven Flusty
Street gangs use spray paint while homeowners
associations use neighborhood watch signs;
either way we are talking informal militias.

9. MVRDV
Due to over-expanding communications networks
and the immeasurable web of inter-relationships
they generate, the world has shed the anachro-
nism "global village" and is transforming into the
more advanced state of the "metacity."

10. Alejandro Zaera-Polo
A high level of density and complexity in the
modes of social, political and economic integration, contemporary urbanity requires high levels
of material complexity.

11. Robert Venturi, Denise Scott Brown, Steven Izenour
Las Vegas space is . . . a new spatial order relating
the automobile and highway communication in
an architecture which abandons pure form in favor
of mixed media.

12. Gilles Deleuze and Félix Guattari
Even the most striated city gives rise to smooth
spaces: to live in the city as a nomad, or as a
cave dweller.

13. Marc Augé
Supermodernity (which stems simultaneously
from the three figures of excess: overabundance
of events, spatial overabundance and the individualization of references) naturally finds its full
expression in non-places.

14. J. G. Ballard
The suburban body has been wholly domesti-
cated, and one can say that the suburbs
constitute a huge petting zoo, with the residents'
bodies providing the stock of furry mammals.

15. Michael Weinstock
We are within the horizon of a systemic change,
from the design and production of individual
"signature" buildings to an ecology in which
evolutionary designs have sufficient intelligence
to adapt and to communicate, and from which
intelligent cities will emerge.

16. Albert Pope
As a form of parasite, the contemporary city pos-
sesses characteristics completely alien to its conventional urban sponsor. What was yesterday an
innocuous extension of conventional form today
turns out to be, not a "suburb," but an entirely
unprecedented type of urban development.

17. Craig Hodgetts
It used to be that E. B. White and the *New Yorker*
held the patent on urbanity, but things have
changed. Contemporary models reject utopian
constructs, and are characterized by their ability to
tolerate dysfunction, conflicts, uncomfortable dis-
parity in scale and texture, and imminent change.

18. Sulan Kolatan

Urbanity is, foremost, a question of lifestyle and "taste-space" now. There are European cities lacking urbanity, and Pacific islands that are extremely urbane. The presence of international airports, fiberoptic cable networks, and roaming cosmopolitan "tribes" sharing overlapping taste-spaces, among others, are indicators of urbanity.

19. Mike Davis

Developers don't grow homes in the desert—this isn't Marrakesh or even Tucson—they just clear, grade and pave hook up some pipes to the local artificial river (the federally subsidized California Aqueduct), build a security wall and plug in the "product."

20. Johan Bettum

Urbanity is in the process of losing its only function: the bringing about of public space. Architects carry no obligation to save it but can do nothing but invest in it. This is not solely a question of scale in terms of space or capital; it is also secured by the scale of our profession's vanity.

21. Tulay Atak

The dictionary defines urbanity as a sensibility, one that seems peculiar to the modern, a certain type of behavior, or even a mannerism. Urbanity might indeed be a sensibility: a "sensibility" toward the city. An architectural urbanity lies in architecture's ability to be influenced and affected by the city, producing deviations in response to the dynamics of it.

22. Reyner Banham

As the car in front turned down the off-ramp of the San Diego freeway, the girl beside the driver pulled down the sun visor and used the mirror on the back of it to tidy her hair. Only when I had seen a few more incidents of this kind did I catch the import: that coming off the freeway is coming in from outdoors.

23. Ari Seligmann

Urban/suburban distinctions and center/periphery dichotomies have been unhinged by the proliferation of uneven terrains of polycentric metropolitan developments, which support increasingly cosmopolitan occupation. A barrage of portmanteau words—"edge cities," "mega-cities," "exopolis," "postmetropolis"—expose the inability to come to terms with contemporary urban conditions. Urbanists ought to demonstrate their urbanity by grasping the potentials of alternative frameworks, especially the perspective of regional agglomerations within global networks and flows.

24. Kevin Lynch

Moving elements in a city, and in particular the people and their activities, are as important as the stationary physical parts. We are not simply observers of this spectacle, but are ourselves a part of it, on the stage with other participants. Most often, our perception of the city is not sustained, but rather partial, fragmentary, mixed with other concerns. Nearly every sense is in operation, and the image is the composite of them all.

25. Benjamin Bratton

Urbanicity is the territory of immeasurable genetic possibility. A fluid density of strange "genetalia," fleshly interfaces to a virtual genomic destiny. It is the spectacle of human complexity and the obtuse cultural capitals it can produce, defend, and endure. It is where you think you are when you move from airport to airport, inert and half-awake: a metabolic contour more than a physiognomy of channels. And finally, it is the orifice through which cargo is transcontinentally transported.

26. Marc Angélil and Sarah Graham

As design processes revolve around questions of becoming, the architectural product could correspondingly be considered in a state of flux. Architecture's material presence, from such a vantage point, cannot be manifested through the design of pristine objects but by the organization of interlaced dynamic systems. Such arrangements need to be open in their structures, leaving room for the possibility of interpretative transformation. In this way, urban formations evolve from a network of relationships in a state of continuous redefinition. An exploration could unfold along two specific lines of development: the first pertains to the formation of flow-surfaces for architectural objects; the second addresses the formation of flow-geometries for field assemblies.

27. Gudrun Hausegger

More than any other term within contemporary architectural discourse, "urbanity" is claimed by diametrically opposed camps. Traditional concepts of urbanity, which have always been linked to the corpus of the city and its specific state of mind, are rapidly transforming. Attempts to preserve these values through commercial developments and the ersatz urbanities of the entertainment industry, or the endeavors of the new urbanism, constitute one end of the spectrum. The other end announces the dissolution of this kind of city, and, in the face of digital networks and global markets, even conceives of the city as completely disengaged from any spatial ties. It is this unresolved tension between the fictive nature of the former, and the projective quality of the latter, that gives rise to the creative friction that will define a distinct urbanity of the future.

28. Diane Favro

The impact of spectacles on urban environments has long been the subject of study; recent interpretations of urbanity have broadened the inquiry to include consideration of the reflexive view, that is, how cityscapes impact events. Ephemeral civic performances have always served to map sites of power and hence, of the city, across both cultural and physical landscapes. When enlivened by a collective spectacle, an urban space is transformed into a performative terrain. Through communal human intervention, the cityscape operates as far more than a passive stage for action. Sequentially or simultaneously, such environments assume the roles of actor, director, or viewer. As a result, performative urban terrains interpret, enrich, and shape human action, literally and conceptually. Only through the consideration of such dependent symbiotic interrelationships can we come to understand the complicated exchange between performances and the urban and cultural terrains they occupy.

29. Michael Bell

While dean at MIT, William Wurster separated the architecture department from the planning department: planners (not trained in design but in economics) would be concerned with policy, while architects would act as designers of buildings. Since the 1990s this division has been eradicated in many architecture schools, and the study of the city (the urban) has become a standard form of inquiry in this nexus. It has become common to describe the postwar city in predatory terms—updating and re-applying themes of alienation—and, from Andre Corboz to Rem Koolhaas, one could say the project of architecture becomes a project of recovery or of subject-building in light of a desperate city. I am not sure urbanity, in my experience, has been about a much wider range of themes: it has not been a theme of sophistication, as in the term "urbane."

30. Helene Furján

The modern city is a site of expansions, tactical and strategic interventions, confrontations between localization and globalization (including shifting cultural identities based on migration patterns), a terrain of constructed space (architectonic and urbanistic), and a map of flows, networks, transfers, and transits (the immaterial images, messages, and vectors of communications and transportations). An urban architecture must acknowledge and respond to the urban condition, proposing new tectonic and structural potentials, models of urban fabrics and dynamic urban strategies, and operational engagements with political and cultural space: architecture embedded within and simultaneously constitutive of the contemporary urban world. The counter side to the city of vectors and circuits of information, exchange, and transit is the *enclave*. Zones of exclusion and homogeneity, enclaves—whether the residential gated and ex-urban developments or the corporate, industrial, or technoscientific compound—produce and operate the logics of control, restriction, privatization, and regulation. As the fastest growing sector of development in the first world, these enclaves reveal the question that nag . . . beneath the city of flows: access.

31. Stan Allen

The late-twentieth century has seen the emergence of a radically horizontal, fieldlike urbanism, driven by the freeway and the suburban ideal of private housing. In the United States, at least, planning has had minimal impact. A new city form has developed, extended in the horizontal dimension, but marked by points of intensity and exchange—nodes where the local thickening of section produces three-D effects within the shallow section of spread-out space of the contemporary city. Cities like Los Angeles have developed as vast, matlike fields, where scattered pockets of density are knit together by high-speed, high-volume roadways. In a more extreme case, in a city like Tokyo, six to ten stories of radically different programs overlap at key transportation interchanges. These radical shifts of scale and extreme social contrast undermine the ability of architecture to mediate transitions.

The experience of the city today is not so much the orderly progression of scales as an experience of rapid shifts in scale and speed of movement. "Section" is created by weaving, superposition, and overlapping, rather than stacking. Today we tend to move with minimal transition from labyrinthine interiors to movement systems: directly from the mall to the freeway. Emergent field effects are visible in unexpected locations: minimalls, freeway interchanges, suburban cinemaplexes, intermodal transportation centers, informal markets in traditional city centers, proliferating fields that mix leisure and recreation, commerce and infrastructure, in unexpected new relationships. In all of these cases, architecture's mediating role becomes increasingly difficult to maintain, and new strategies are required. At the intersection of architecture, landscape, and urbanism, a new field is emerging.

Quality of being urbane: refined, elegant, suavity. Sophisticated life in major cities.

This general definition of urbanity refers to "people" in cities, not the city (the built form) itself. One imagines that a sophisticated life is comprised of a broad array of specific cultural concerns, such as food, literature, art, education, human interaction, etc., the totality of which is a deeply saturated and rich lifestyle, accentuated by the dual modes of ritual and spontaneity. The metropolitan experience is indeed a life of programmatic density with the thriving, visceral built environment as a backdrop to the millions of individual pathways articulated by bodies moving in space. However, *urbanity* is not a term that today is limited to the description of an erudite person motivated by a certain need for high-end culture(s). In fact, the language system of architecture has adapted the term *urbanity* as an extension of the more frequently used *urban*, or *urbanism*, terms that refer directly to cities and their structures. This is a curious shift in meaning, one that has withered away the connotations of suavity and elegance in favor of scale, mass, material complexity, and perhaps, sheer power. Life in cities is surely still analyzed in terms of social and economic stratifications, but *urbanity*, as it is now used, is an inclusive term, one that perhaps tends to destratify culture, dissolve its "layers," and more fluidly pour it back into the structure of the city.

Given that the human, social content of the city is now a more fluxual "plasma," not so easily dominated by the upper levels of the educated class, the term *urbanity* no doubt refers implicitly to the types of city organizations, i.e., accumulations of built form that have arisen over time, especially in the 20th century when transportation and information/communication systems began to dramatically change the relative coordinates of time and distance. During this time, when major world cities began to change from centralized agglomerations to vastly more peripheral webs becoming inversely less identifiable, new terms were invented to describe the hybridization of urban and suburban networks. Indeed, the "metropolitan" became the "metroplex," the "city" became the "region," and still further, the "suburban" became the "ex-urban." If the urban is now a supercomplex, fluid matrix of control systems within a deep field, where inert material has given way to flows of all kinds, could it be possible that "urbanity" now refers not only to urban structures, but rather to the temporal organizations of people using knowledge and position via technology? This may well be the most accurate way of describing, once again, how people define urbanity. Whether moving along the freeway, within the www, in the flow of subterranean transportation, in a trancelike lotus position, or in a café with newspaper and novel in hand, it is safe to assume that the position in communications space has become more important than one's position in a refined social system. Indeed, it is the refinement and evolution of technology that has rewritten urban codes.

Perhaps the computer nerd is the new urban sophisticate after all.

URBANITY

GEOMETRY

Don't be
square

1. Sanford Kwinter

Topology . . . describes *transformational events* (deforma- tions) that introduce real discontinuities into the evolution of the system itself.

GEOMETRY

2. Jesse Reiser

Distinct from classical Euclidean geometry, [topological] geometries develop potentials to engage flows in living and non-living systems.

3. Alejandro Zaera-Polo

Geometry is the most promising contemporary domain of architectural theory and the most operative region of contemporary architectural practice

4. Michael Bell

No topic has been more influential nor more fully turned upside down and inside out by rapid developments of use than geometry.

5. Thom Mayne

One could argue that there's only geometry. a building merely operates in time and space within the mathematical and geographical condition of its formation.

6. Greg Lynn

The next step involves the development of an abstract model of complexity. Throughout the history of philosophy, geometry has been invoked to accomplish this task.

7. Mark C. Taylor

Several important conclusions follow from the attempt to revive morphology. First, and most obviously, the organism cannot be understood as the sum of its parts but must be considered *as a whole*.

8. Ben van Berkel and Peter Trümmer

If you intensify certain aspects of the organisation of a geometry, such as the Möbius belt, other aspects, such as the distribution of the program, the construction and the routing, are also intensified.

9. Cecil Balmond

The *informal* has three principal characteristics: local, hybrid and juxtaposition. They are active ingredients of an animate geometry that embraces the linear and non-linear. Both Cartesian and post-Einsteinian geometry are encompassed by it.

10. Gilles Deleuze and Félix Guattari

The line escapes geometry by a fugitive mobility at the same time as life tears itself free from the organic by a permutating, stationary whirlwind. This vital force specific to the Abstraction is what draws smooth space.

11. Jeffrey Kipnis

Experimenting with computer "morphing" programmes that smoothly transform one figure into another, or employing topological meshing techniques such as splines, NURBS, etc. that join the surfaces delimited by the perimeters of disjoint two-dimensional figures into a smoothed solid.

12. Johan Bettum

Orthogonal and Euclidean codes represent an outmoded economic and political reality rather than an architectural one. The idea of an absolute and "perfect" geometry belongs to the past and does not inscribe the radical rupture that we now desire.

13. Michael Hensel and Kivi Sotama

The differentiated geometry of the material construct and the changing intensities of ambient affects, as well as the individual and collective movement of visitors and performers, continually converged and diverged, provisionally assembling and dispersing the elements of the intervention into ever-changing configurations.

14. Heather Roberge

Geometries that are designed to carry certain techniques and tactics within them describe flows, effects, and atmospheres that are much closer to their own constitution, moving beyond passive description into a condition that is partially real. These more dynamic geometries allow us to work in that elusive zone that exists between the diagram and the building.

15. Jason Payne

Matter is intimately tied to its own geometry, to its own descriptive devices. There is a difference between looking at a cloud and either seeing a unicorn or seeing a vector field. There's nothing wrong with seeing a unicorn, but to actually work with a cloud's substance, as opposed to its image, you have to work with its vector field.

16. Russell Fortmeyer

Geometry is a formal vocabulary established to abstract and simplify the natural world in the pursuit of a pure order of the relations between things. Architects rely on geometry as the principal means for communicating a design. It has undergone a radical reexamination in the past fifty years, but attempts to dislodge geometry as the essential language of architecture remain largely experimental and unsuccessful.

17. Craig Hodgetts

Geometry is a means of describing shapes in such a way that they may be precisely duplicated. The nature of the shape—scribble, blob, Euclidean solid, or tessellation—is irrelevant to the discipline. What I find personally satisfying is that the computer has reduced the perspiration that must have filled buckets in Eiffel's case to picoliters of it accumulated at the tip of a finger.

18. Michael Weinstock

Geometry has a subtle role in morphogenesis. It is necessary to think of the geometry of a biological or computational form not only as the description of the fully developed form, but also as the set of boundary constraints that act as a local organising principle for self-organisation during morphogenesis. Pattern and feedback are as significant in the models of morphogenesis as they are in the models of cybernetics and dynamic systems.

19. R. E. Somol

I don't find that the touchstone of architecture lies in its geometric identity. The procedural difficulty of its formal emergence, or in terms of indexing some condition, only can be expressed by geometry. For those who perfect the so-called rigors of form, geometry is the raison d'être of architecture. For me, it's merely an expedient device toward other material, programmatic, and contextual effects: thus, I opt for the modern, slackened condition of shape, not the classical metaphysics of form.

20. Ann Bergren

From early Greece comes a definition of the beautiful that supplants arguments about form alone: the poet Sappho claims, "Some say an array of horsemen, others, of foot soldiers, others, of ships, is the most beautiful thing on earth, but I say it is that for which you have erotic love." An "erotics" of formal choice—asking of each aesthetic judgment what social drives, what personal history, what political aims make up my "eros" here—brings out of geometry, the measurer and generator of now virtually any shape and space, its essential role as ethical instrument.

21. Greg Lynn

As Robin Evans said more than a decade ago, architects do not make things; they make *drawings* of things. Geometry transmits information about shape, dimension, assembly, and connection between physical building components. Due to the need to precisely measure form, simple mathematics has limited geometries used by architects to whole numbers, points, lines, radii, and Platonic volumes—cubes, pyramids, spheres, cylinders, planes and circles. With the availability of calculating devices, topological geometries—such as surfaces constructed from networks of spline curves—become possible, based on complex calculus equations too cumbersome today without the assistance of computers.

22. Jesse Reiser

Rather than using analogy and proportion to measure the building, sublimating it to an abstract geometry, the use of strands in modeling and diagrams that build an intensity or radiance permits the exploration of a set of connected relationships, precise but, as yet, without number or materiality. That diagram requires conversion to a scale at some point—say, the *strands* become centerlines for space-frame elements—but ultimately the strands vanish from the project, replaced by other systems of repetition working along their grains. Strands and other patterns are amenable to differentiation in a way that the more reduced manipulations of an abstract plane forbid; they have a finer grain of scale and order.

GEOMETRY

23. Michael Bell

Topology, a near-ubiquitous term by the mid-1990s, retained its fundamental value in the face of over use. Robert Slutzky and Joan Ockman's 1984 essay "Color, Structure, Painting" suggested that Slutzky's paintings "turn space inside out" like a torus glove: figure and field were made "simultaneously one." The term *torus* is now in common use—as is Mobius strip, Klein Bottle, and even Hypersphere. But the wider revolution of fusing geometry and algebraic equations—of topology—is still in its infancy in architecture. Linked to historically essential drawing techniques such as figure/ground it opens up themes like inside-out houses and other operations that break down the questionable concept of interiority. Nevertheless, topological geometry remains underdeveloped in its ability to negotiate production and perception.

24. Greg Lynn

Geometry is often considered to be complete in itself. Like the theory of gravity—now heatedly debated in conferences by theoretical physicists, astronomers, and engineers—it is simplistically assumed that the question of geometry was solved in the sixteenth century. "You can't ignore gravity" is the mantra of those with no knowledge of contemporary thoughts on gravity, weight, and structure. Today, while there is an exciting interest in form, shape, material, lighting, mood, and ambience, there is a distinct lack of intellectual curiosity in the rigorous medium of architecture: that is, in geometry.

Geometry is not only dimension, the reverse engineering of expressionist form; geometry connotes the intricate relationships between the mass and the component, between the elements that necessarily are assembled together to form larger scale solids, voids, spaces, and surfaces. Geometry supplies the possibility for synthesis, wholism, scalar transformation, harmony, proportion, and the other characteristics associated with discourses of classical beauty in architecture. The prevalent lack of attention to the rigors of geometry is neither a distaste for it, nor a 1980s slackness in the face of authority but, more pointedly, a distrust of the project of beauty. Geometry may be derided as the messenger of a passé and impossible model of beatific order convoluted by mannerists, purified by modernists, debased by neoclassicists, and overrated by process-driven pseudo-scientists. Nonetheless, geometry is an aspect of the architectural medium to be exploited.

Geometrical rigor is a central aspect of our medium, distinguishing architecture from painting, sculpture, interior design, and many other fields with which architecture shares techniques. Some geometries may be difficult while others might be bankrupt; geometric manipulation may come more easily for some than for others and, yes, geometry is a matter of taste. Every architect needs to pose the question of what kind of geometry is associated with his or her architecture; this can be explicit or implicit but the problem is posed every time we draw.

25. Preston Scott Cohen

It is possible today for the architect to conceive of a precise relationship—one, moreover, that is wholly unprecedented—between the configurations of geometry and architecture, a relationship marked by mutual agitation and reciprocal alteration. But at present, this remains a provisional hypothesis. Foundationalist nostalgias aside, it must be admitted that without a firm conception of the epistemological grounds of architecture, no such inventive agitation can take place. For, unlike previous periods when this kind of interaction was able to develop, the absolute foundations of architecture and geometry can no longer be taken for granted.

To begin a new project involving a fertile agitation of architectural forms by means of geometry, it is useful to look at advancements in geometry that began during the Renaissance. The development of seventeenth-century projective geometry can be traced in part to this period when there were indications of an alternative vision of the architecture/geometry interaction: the instrumental, technical advancements in representation and construction—perspective, orthogonal projection, axonometry, stereotomy. This vision could not be realized in practical terms in the succeeding two centuries because projective geometry in the seventeenth century and descriptive geometry at the end of the eighteenth were disembodied and disassociated from architecture. While Renaissance architecture required axiality and grids to manifest hierarchical, centralized forms through perspectival convergence, projective geometry, for the most part, advanced remotely from the space and discipline of architecture.

Between the Baroque era and the Enlightenment we see two connected developments: the codification of these forms of geometric knowledge—the period that gave birth to the means of intersection between cylinders, cones, ellipsoids, and spheres—and in architecture, the gradual disappearance of nonorthogonal forms as a reflection of the commitment to programmatic standards. The result for architecture was that basic shapes predominated, and in the nineteenth century, though complex geometric techniques were taught to architects, they were hardly used by them. It was in the field of engineering that the techniques of intersection, enabled by stereotomy and projective geometry, were used for the design of machines, ships, trains, etc. In the twentieth century these forms would be transferred back into architecture as iconography and analogy (as opposed to geometric technique) mimicked as a new "machine aesthetic."

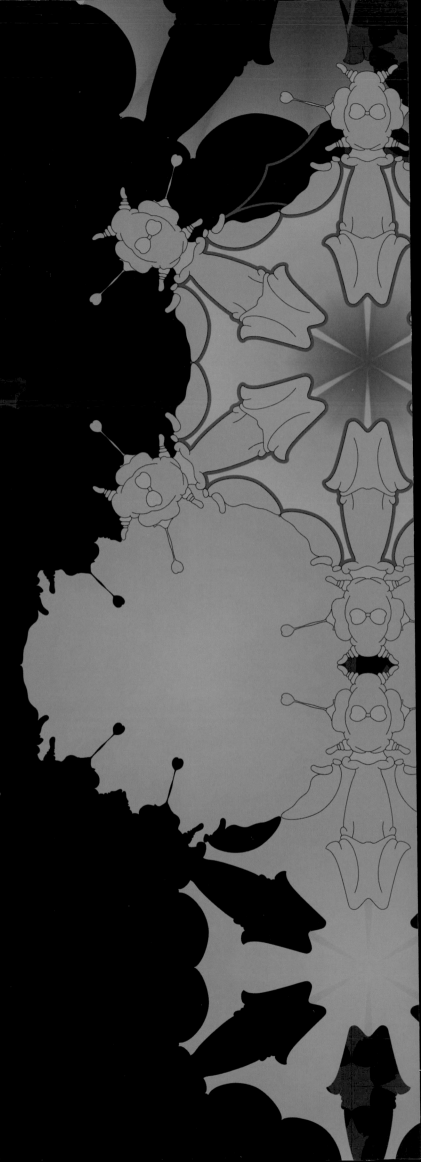

There have been several other nostalgic revisions to geometry as an iconographic program in architecture. The fragmentary forms of Deconstructivism set against normative elements such floors and structural components—thought by architects and theorists to be necessitated by developing technologies, or by the fluidity and indeterminacy of modern life—remain as arbitrary, vague, or imprecise as the compositional methods that lead to "normal" architecture. The claims that these developments are inevitable, and necessary or due to advancing technologies in our time are spurious. Indeed, I would argue, those who seek to guarantee the legitimacy of architecture through such claims behave as if they are metaphysicians. Nevertheless, among academic architects today, there is a movement afoot that maintains that the changing circumstances of contemporary life find their implicit architectural equivalence in the form of a blob.

Would it be possible for digital media to shift the emphasis from the iconographic programs of architecture to the development of alternative methodological foundations? True, architecture cannot provide axiomatic foundations comparable to those of complex geometry. Nevertheless, it is possible today to recognize the autonomy of geometry, and to understand the consequences of disrupting it according to the circumstances of architectural conventions. For example, can the architect intervene in the world of inviolable geometric autonomy? Can the arbitrary (conventional) lines and spatial divisions of practical Euclidean forms merge with the necessary lines and spatial indivisibility of nonorientable geometric figures and their linear intersections? By seeking similar degrees of surface curvature between independent geometric figures—primitive forms such as cones, spheres, cylinders on the one hand, and nonorientable self-intersecting rectangles, self-intersecting one-sided surfaces such as helicoids, and catenoids, on the other—near-tangencies can be achieved, invoking a possible but ultimately unattainable synthesis. This discord parallels the perennial disagreement between geometry and materiality. Only now, what happens to the relationship between inside and outside? How do we contend with this problem programmatically? What are the thermal and material implications and consequences? Finally, do these conditions need to be shaped explicitly or inexplicitly, according to geometric principles that beg these questions? It is the promise of order and the evident struggle undertaken to realize it that is of interest. Perhaps there will be a new "near miss" between the disciplines, another iteration in the ongoing contest: architecture v. geometry.

GEOMETRY

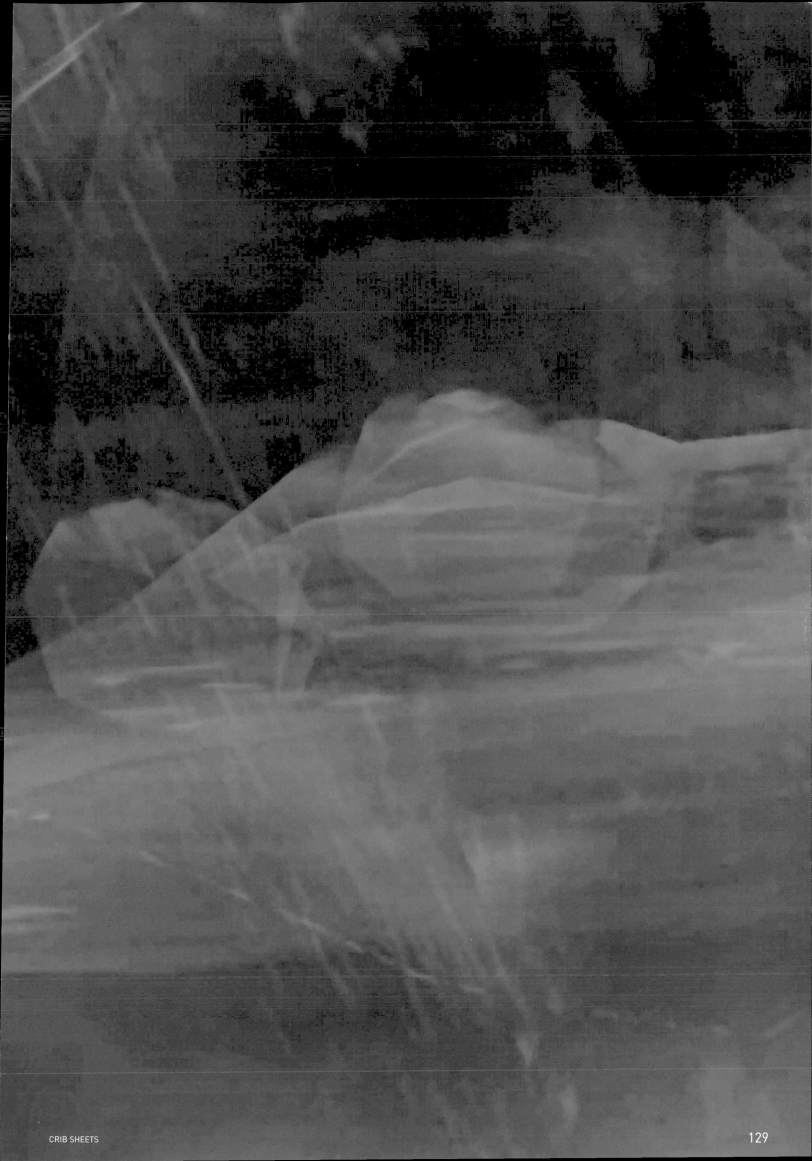

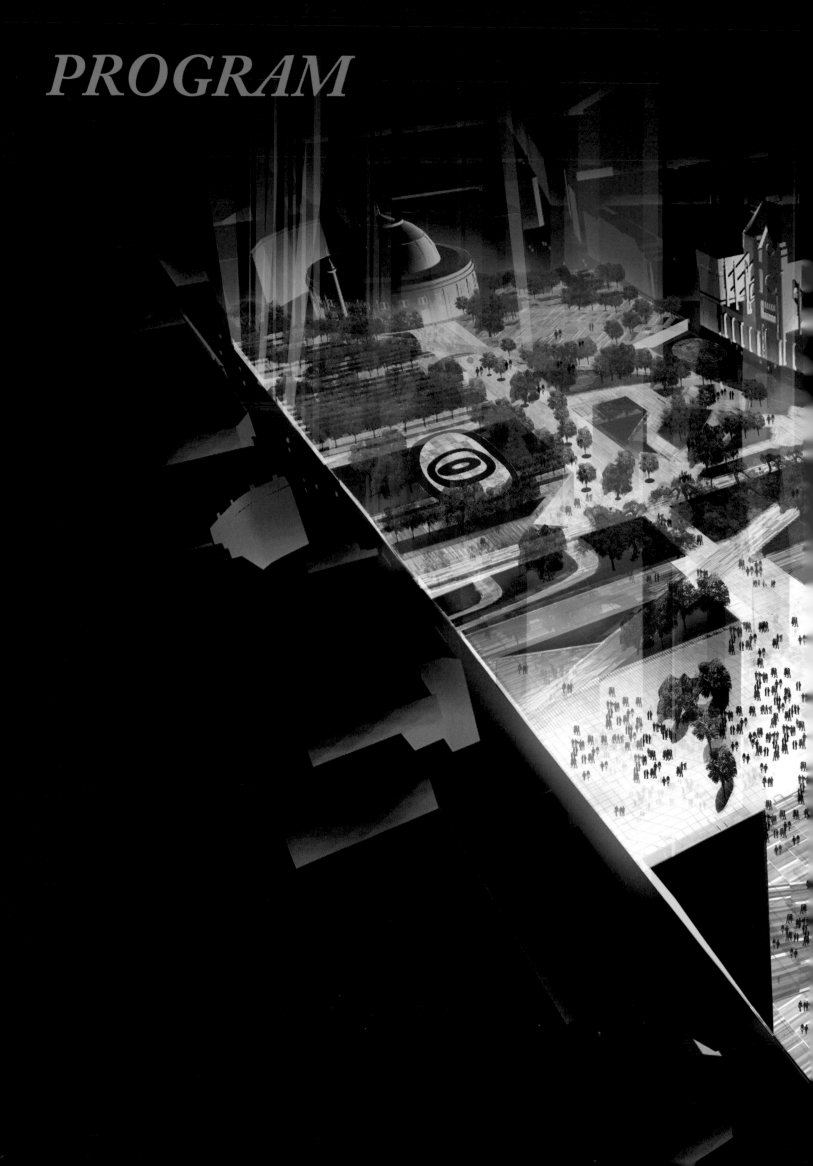

PROGRAM

Do not try this at home

Program is the most politically correct side of architecture's double agenda of performances

PROGRAM

2. Richard Neutra
Function may itself be a follower—for example, when form and color excite sex in courtship.

3. Craig Hodgetts
Architecture as a machine is multivalence-trumps-specificity, the illusion of the needs of a dynamic (thus successful) entity.

4. Peter Eisenman
[Post-functionalism] changes the humanist balance of form/function to a dialectical relationship within the evolution of form itself.

5. Jesse Reiser
The loose fit between programme and form is acknowledged, and subsequently the lack of priority of the former over the latter.

6. William Gibson
Tattoo parlors, gaming arcades, dimly lit stalls stacked with decaying magazines, sellers of fireworks, of cut bait, betting shops, sushi bars, unlicensed pawnbrokers, herbalists, barbers, bars.

7. Ben van Berkel and Peter Trümmer
The double-locked torus of the Möbius house illustrates how the idea of the two inhabitants and the two materials is caught in a diagram, which subsequently is transformed into a specific structural effect.

8. Robert Venturi, Denise Scott Brown, Steven Izenour
The intricate maze under the low ceiling never connects with outside light or outside space. This disorients the occupant in space and time. He loses track of where he is and when it is.

9. Raymond M. Hood
Whole industries should be united into interdependent developments with clubs, hotels, stores, apartments and even theaters. Such an arrangement would make possible great economies in time, as well as diminish wear and tear on human nerves.

10. Rem Koolhaas
Rockefeller Center is the most mature demonstration of Manhattanism's unspoken theory of the simultaneous existence of different programs on a single site, connected only by the common data of elevators, service cores, columns and external envelope.

11. Greg Lynn
The variations in the global form result from local variations in the program, and these variations are taken up in a repetitive construction technique in which every element is slightly differentiated within a more or less continuous system.

12. MVRDV
Incising and stretching the parking volume required in the brief, carves out enormous "recesses" between the parking layers, offering space for shops, supermarkets, medical facilities, a social/cultural centre, a library, a church, a sports hall and some eighty houses.

13. Charles Jencks
The emphasis on the program, John Summerson argued, distinguished modernism from previous architectures. Program subsumed function and narrative and was meant to turn the architect into a visionary social engineer. Perhaps only dystopias like Brasilia and Celebration were actually built by architects, but social imagination—changing the given program—remains one of the most potent sources of creative architecture today.

14. R. E. Somol
We can stipulate that every designed object has programmatic and formal effects. For instance, Greg Lynn's tea set for Alessi will have programmatic or "use" effects, whether that's how it was generated or otherwise. The question is, where do you want the significant effects to lie, which ones do you want to provisionally be obligated to, what establishes the architectural project?

15. Sylvia Lavin

The migration of this evolving form clearly defies the idea that form should follow function and exposes a kind of semi-autonomy in the relation of form and program. Indeed, [Gehry's Horse's Head] has resisted the moralistic tyranny of program-driven architecture by developing a tactical rather than essentializing attitude toward program and context, and a plastic rather than causal relation between function and form.

16. Stan Allen

The extended horizontal surface—architecture's plan dimension—is the primary support for program. Hence terms like "battlefield" or "sports field" indicate the idea of the *field* as the support for complex interactive events unfolding in time. However, it is not only the field that supports programmatic complexity; landscape has its own spatial vocabulary (matrix, corridors, and patches, for example) that describes movement, connectivity, and exchange.

17. Benjamin Bratton

Programs—architectural, televisual, computational, political programs, and so on—anticipate repetition in advance of themselves, and condition this as the arrangement of space and flow. Because habits wear grooves into the surfaces of habitat, to propose a collective habit's *becoming*— "this is what we should do"—is to propose a collective habitat's program—"this is how/where we should do it." The activation of program is a performance of, and/or against, this condition, now revealed as a continuity of mimetic formation, evasion, and incomprehension.

18. Johan Bettum

Program is persistently deployed as a predetermined and finite set of activities affiliated with and coded for an equally fixed set of material forms and functional types. In short, programming remains poorly understood and highly underestimated as an instrumental and temporal construct through which prescribed and nonprescribed activities are synthesized in physical form. No building has ever presented a finite agenda for human occupation. Once architects are able to fathom this in a practical sense will we see programming develop as accretion and substratum, namely the horizon of event structures.

19. Preston Scott Cohen

An ant grows a cone not because of personal existential dilemmas associated with its own creation but because of a programmatic condition. Frank Lloyd Wright tried to invent a new way to exhibit an emerging medium—nonobjective art—which mutated a paradigm of the museum, fusing incompatible models that were a curiosity in the linear sequence of galleries, an emergence that wasn't instrumentally devised according to the program he set out to deal with. This exemplifies another relationship exists between programmatic cause and formal effect: deviation or anomaly.

20. Greg Lynn

Function refers to the manner in which architecture is used. *Program* is the means by which a building's function takes on an institutional and symbolic value, and is eventually representational, while *function* is not necessarily this—the minute a building's function takes on an institutional valence it becomes program. In this way, program affiliates with aesthetics in a complex and often covert manner. This explains the preponderance of functional analysis that is turned into form, as well as the inability for architects to make aesthetic claims for their work without recourse to functional explanation.

21. Alice Friedman

The program is not only a document that records the desired functions of spaces in a building or the required adjacencies or patterns of circulation. It is much more than that: exceeding the literal and the visual, the program encodes relationships between the representation of power and shapes through formal design strategies and planning solutions. It is a virtual record, combining written and unwritten (conscious and unconscious) information, which describe the ideologies that shape architectural form, drawing on and reifying attitudes toward gender, sexuality, and the status of social and political institutions. For historians of architecture and urban form, the program is the starting point for research and analysis; it holds the key to understanding the evolution of design and the operations of spatial systems within a matrix of cultural values.

22. Michael Bell

Program has become operational—and in the hands of architects like Stan Allen, Stanley Saitowitz, or Mark Wamble it has become a time-based form of human geometry that has supplanted an operational or transformation project of form. Bernard Tschumi continues to be a foundation for and an essential footnote to the term *program*—there is "no architecture without program"—and the Manhattan Transcripts is still the Situationist set of events that establishes Columbia's stage for work on the "event" rather than form. Program has been reinvented again as a device or sector of emergent behavior—instead of solving the program, an architect who sees program through a lens provided by Tschumi (or Guy Debord or René Thom) sees it as a form of generative crisis. This is not the programming of *Time Saver Standards* or the fated operations of a mid-century form-follows-function. Here, program is the *becoming* of the building.

23. Neil Denari

Program: a plan of action or a set of predetermined names of rooms? The first might be called *ideology*, *argument*, or *set-up*, presumably the most important set of instructions an architect can work with. The second could be called a *catalyst*, something that brings about form to a plan of action, as in the polymerization process in epoxy resin. *Ideology* is predicated on editing possibilities, on setting up a sequence of events, quite often exiling the normative program to the heap of countless other banalities that riddle experimental architecture. However, if design gains power by invoking not only cultural possibilities but also the logic of use (which includes both common sense and "ingenious" interpretations of function), then what the building does and how it works is not simply a question of "What is your argument?" or "What kind of building is this?" It is an interactive mix of both, each unable to catalyze one without the other.

24. Jesse Reiser

Program is an order word, a semantic determinant of what is nominally said to happen in a space, but we all know that what really happens is often quite different. Institutions attach to program as part of the "social contract." People agree to abide by programmatic "orders" when they engage with the institution, even though objectively that form of conduct is not reducible to the architecture itself. The institution may very well change over time, and so, too, the practice. When the basis of architectural design puts program in the foreground, then the assumption is that novelty is only possible through programmatic invention. As a consequence of that ideology, when you encounter normative program you get a normative architecture; its formal dimension is invisible and remains unexamined and inert. Then architecture is about inventing novel programmatic combinations. In these cases, all the elements are already known, and the result can be properly called *combinatorial*, not innovative. Most of the time, as architects, we do not have the opportunity to invent programs. Does that mean that architecture is doomed? We would say no.

The modernist model of office space in which space represents its function, for example, has transformed into a newer model where hardware becomes more dematerialized and space no longer needs to correlate to function, permitting experiments in which offices are transformed into lounges whose appeal lies in atmosphere. Once the representation of function is jettisoned, other aspects of space come to the fore, making it function better. The effects of materiality, which aren't merely aesthetic, are the kind of indirect influences that might attract certain programs, or even a range of programs. Better to imply a range of activities that could occur within a space than to spell them out.

25. Dana Cuff

Program, like *site*, is a term that endures in architectural practice, yet is hardly mentioned in theoretical discourse. By contrast, *site* has been resuscitated through landscape, and as such offers new formal paradigms as well as new discursive ones. Not so the program, which persists in its conscribed role as a reference document by which clients communicate square footage requirements to guide the architect. There is no inherent reason why program cannot transcend its instrumentality, but to do so requires conceptual reframing.

If by program we mean the narrative an architect constructs for a building to foreshadow the life it will eventually house, then program at some fundamental level depends upon our ideas about what constitutes a good "story" and how good we are at telling it. These ideas have changed rather drastically over the past few decades. In 1979, Colin Rowe set up what was in fact a straw man when he contrasted paradigm with program, arguing that the latter was incapable of generating new architectural form. He was relying on a conventional notion that equates program with the pragmatic, functional requirements. Deriving from empirical positivist science, this program is definable and measurable—as well as dull. Environmental social scientists trooped into schools, mental health wards, public parks, and private bathrooms to engineer a perfect fit between human factors and environmental design. They were armed with confidence that behavioral data was at the heart of sociospatial action, from codes of privacy to defensible space. Their narratives made public housing as systematically intelligible as a car's dashboard, and a good telling comprised well-analyzed data.

Rowe's intention was to separate architecture from the deterministic bondage conjoining modernist functionalism to Skinnerian logic. His opposing model, a conceptual and autonomously governed architecture, was at the time already taking hold. Program was part and parcel of building's semiotic meaning, from roadside ducks to Charles Moore and Michael Graves. Both linguistics and historicism were pertinent to an architecture in which program was more like poché than anything formally generative. Program, in postmodern narratives, was subsumed by the typological: the fifteenth-century palazzo retains its form even when it is converted over the centuries to a hospital, and later, residential apartments. Theoretically, function, use—or better—ritual, along with form, were mere surface perturbations of type's deep structure.

As the program's intellectual bearings shifted, architects and clients paid no attention, writing programs as always, developing and abiding by standards for everything from the school child's minimum playground allotment to the number of parking spaces that must accompany a two-bedroom apartment. While social practices can be codified into regulation or legitimated by empirical data, program can also be seen as another manifestation of fashion in architecture. Instead, what if the postmodern program, like functionalism that preceded it, is just a way we once explained the world? Before, Graves was our Margaret Mead, Portland our Samoa. Built on well-told narratives, the views they rendered described a world no longer accessible; the exoticism each portrayed then is now slightly embarrassing. A postmodern office building tells us about the prevailing standards for architecture, and looking at it, we see a sublimated program. Among contemporary anthropologists, cultural narratives are appreciated for their poetics, as well as their facticity, ethnographic writing being recognized as a practice in itself, as culturally driven as aboriginal painting. Program is thus a social construction, and as such can be theorized and aestheticized as well as practiced.

Now architects, in a recent programmatic twist, make datascapes. When these are intended to legitimate observations, converting them to facts, they resort to Rowe's first notion of program. They are useful primarily as propaganda, to convince the powers that be that the architect controls the "facts." But when datascapes become poetic, elegant, cool, or smart in their own right, then we can see the emergence of a newly invigorated program. FOA's Yokohama ferry terminal and van Berkel's Mobius House were spun from smart narratives that became part of the productive material for architecture. MVRDV's function-mixers, Massumi's biograms, mass customization, time-use diagrams—in each is a new narrative of the program, created within instrumental contexts but with conceptual and theoretical implications. As these models evolve, what remains to be done is to bring them into relation with one another, discursively and practically, so that their independent possibilities contribute to more than a single building or firm. Only then will program assume a new paradigmatic and critical role in design.

PROGRAM

One small step for mankind

This book must no longer be filed under Technology.

2. Jesse Reiser
There are no flows without matter, and no matter without flows.

3. Paul Virilio
From now on, urban architecture must deal with the advent of a "technological space-time."

4. Chris Wise
Is emergent technology investigation or creation? Do these processes start with us or finish with us?

5. Mark Goulthorpe
Technology, or technological change, is most essentially a stretching of cognitive aptitude to assimilate a changed technical standard.

6. Richard Neutra
Magic wanes as technology advances but some of the "old" is saved as ornament to warm the heart.

7. Buckminster Fuller
My ideas have undergone a process of emergence by emergency. When they are needed badly enough, they are accepted.

8. Steven Johnson
Technology analysts never tire of reminding us that pornography is the ultimate early adopter... But video games are challenging that old adage.

9. Ellen Lupton
Botox injections allow a small dose of the toxin that causes botulism to paralyze selected facial muscles, easing wrinkles caused by habitual frowning and eyebrow-raising.

10. Guy Julier
New technologies have allowed a partial "democratization" of design through allowing access to its tools: tasks which were once the preserve of trained specialists now become almost menial.

11. Michael Hensel and Kivi Sotama
The role of technology must be rethought as both substrate and catalyst for new types of dynamic and divergent production processes, with performativity being its condition and aim.

12. Anthony Vidler
"*L'homme-type*," the modulor muscleman, has through a combination of prosthetic devices, drugs, and body sculpture emerged as Cyborg, a potentially gender-free mutant, and its home is no longer a house.

13. Benjamin Bratton
Technology is a condition whereby the repetition of assembly organizes a durable instrument, the image of the component, and the compulsion of mediation. It is the means by which the goals of utility becomes machinic fiction.

14. Adrian Franklin
Using "new small batch technologies" designers were able to avoid the unprofitable depths of the mass market by designing things very specifically to lifestyle groups and, in so doing, further defining and redefining the groups themselves.

15. Servo
The coupling of technology with the atmospheric, compounded by the influence of the computational, is relevant to architectural production and practice today: these modes of operation are ubiquitous in the contemporary environment, from the urban to the individual human scale.

16. Johan Bettum
The proliferation of technology in the production of architecture, as much as in the architectural object, is not merely a sign of the times; it is the surfeit of material practice, an expression of the desire to manifest machinic moments in human effort.

17. Dawn Finley and Mark Wamble
To suggest architectural design excellence begins and ends with matters of fabrication would diminish architecture as an effective force of enlightenment and change. Likewise, to marginalize issues of fabrication as merely technical would limit the level at which buildings of complexity are treated.

18. Dana Cuff
New technology removes the subject (including the maker) in ways that previous technological developments didn't. The Ford Taurus, for example, may be about the buyer and the market, but it's also about what the computer can produce, what a certain kind of software and technology is capable of making.

19. Frank Gehry
Since we discovered the CATIA software program . . . [Dassault Systèmes has been] working on making the system fit our way of working. So they now have a new enhanced CATIA that they're going to install here, which backs us up even more and allows us to control the architectural processes to within seven decimal points of accuracy.

20. Michael Hensel
We are at the threshold of having multiparametric digital tools that generate and analyse combined geometric, structural, material, spatial and habitational characteristics and capacities. In combination with computer-aided manufacturing tools, such as rapid prototyping, physical models of selected transition states can be produced and tested in actual or simulated environments and the test data can be fed back into the generative process in the digital environment.

21. Jason Payne
The computer-generated wire-frame model is the best thing to happen to architecture in years. We're beginning to see physical models—and buildings, by extension—regain substance, as they become more "aware" of their own latent "wire frames." By this I mean the visualization of resistances and rhythms generated across flows of matter and information. Ultimately there is no fundamental difference between physical and digital form when it's understood in terms of matter.

22. Sanford Kwinter
Few people would disagree that our civilization, our ethics and our politics are through and through technological ones. And yet the horror lies not here, but in the fact that we, as beings, as animals, as examples of a once human *nature*, are so fully and irretrievably technological ourselves that we are today deprived of a language with which to articulate, even to summon a memory of, the historical passage towards this fate which has claimed us.

23. Sulan Kolatan
Remarkably, computer-aided design and manufacturing software now constitute cross-platforms, from which such diverse products as coffee machines, running shoes, cars, films, virtual and physical environments, and architecture, are being launched. In other words, the tools for making and the processes of mental and material creation can no longer be assumed to differ fundamentally among product categories of the man-made. Contemporary theory and practice, in our view, has no choice but to concern itself with this "generative convergence" and its consequences. The established methods of generation and terms of classification of so-called second nature must be reevaluated.

24. Michael Bell
Rafael Moneo, writing about Aldo Rossi in *Oppositions*, tested the potential limits of Rossi's search for what he termed the "specificity of the discipline of architecture." Moneo sought the principles that Rossi argued allowed the city to be constructed and "produced from architecture," and that required Rossi to maintain an evasiveness towards the role technology played in the construction of the contemporary city. This "amnesia," according to Moneo, allowed Rossi to maintain a belief that architecture could indeed provide "urban facts" appropriate to their territorializing power to the forces of technology, communications, and capital, which have long superceded cartographic borders and local territories. Fundamental to a new generation's relationship to technology is a shift from this "amnesia": technology is more and more in the hands of the architect and the computational tools of the 1990s have made this possible.

25. Greg Lynn
The introduction of a new technology into a design field has a very different effect from that of the introduction of technology into a scientific or engineering field. In the former, it acts to render designers amateurs, as it often implies new techniques and methods. For the latter, on the other hand, it often solves previously intractable problems. The automotive industry, as an example, raises several points, the first concerning the question of paradigm: if the Ford Taurus is a breakwater project for the automobile industry, what is the equivalent in architecture? The second lies in the technology and design-vocabulary transfer from the auto industry into architecture. The computer is technologically central to both these design fields today for a number of reasons: it provides new formal and geometrical potential; initially de-skills designers, and demands a new kind of design expertise in the digital medium; it provides an acceleration, design, and manufacture of objects; it makes initial designs more accurate and precise earlier in the process; it makes mass-produced objects in smaller batches; and, as a result, accelerates the quantity of design objects. These issues, which are germane to the new digital medium, are making disparate design fields more similar than they have ever been.

TECHNOLOGY

26. Jesse Reiser

The relationship between invention and necessity is particularly interesting. Rather than grounding our work in culture and deriving our practice from a reading of existing practices, with their contradictions, and so on, we affirm the productivity of invention in itself. The history of technology bears this out. In a chapter of *Guns, Germs, and Steel*, the anthropologist Jared Diamond offers a "reverse logic" of technological invention. The phonograph, for example, went through a series of failed incarnations (i.e., as a means of recording the last words of the dying, etc.) before it was taken up in the productive assemblage of music recording. Only retrospectively are the relationships necessary and inevitable. Indeed, this dimension of the unforeseen is important both in the way we conceive our work and also in how it will be utilized.

The symptoms of such invention, in the case of the Flux Room, could be, and have been, appropriated by new media, as well as by musicians. The way the "flows" are scripted includes all the elements of music, in the sense that they deal with a quantity, a modulation, and a timeline. This development is precisely interdisciplinary because it involves the building of generic systems the content of which is supplied or worked on by others. This is the proper role of the interdisciplinary architect, analogous to the preparation of a site. This is the field on which architecture is most potent, at the level of context, substrate, infrastructure, and ground for the life and practices of others. We do not presume to overdetermine the practices or that form of interpretive, representative content.

27. Craig Hodgetts

From athletic shoes to laser surgery, our high-gain culture emphasizes speed over deliberation, the envelope over the enclosure, global positioning over mapping, and the dynamic over the static: the tune-up over the rundown; the hum over the grunt; performance, performance, performance.

However, technology has only recently become a partner in the production of architecture. Adventurous architecture in times past had only a passing acquaintance with the developing technology of its time. Architecture has always been a technological wallflower, binding architects to static arrangements based on gravitational attraction and surface elaboration. That is, until recently, when an explosion of computational tools and visualization techniques invite architects to take the floor with the industrial designers and engineers who have traditionally advanced manufacturing technology for use in the production of aircraft and vehicles.

A few hundred years ago, while Leonardo was musing about helicopters and spring-powered vehicles, and Vaucason was building a clockworks-driven robot, buildings were still constructed by piling stone on stone, and the big deal was Brunelleschi's use of a chain to rein in the tension forces of his dome. It could be argued that, aside from insights into the laws of statics, every structure up to and including the Monadnock Building could have been constructed within the technologic boundaries that existed before the birth of Christ. Stylistic variations were on the order of automotive tail fins and applied trim—visual elaborations that did nothing to challenge the known parameters of their type. Technology transfer, for architects, began when John Bogardus adopted casting methods that had long been used for factory equipment and domestic appliances to the framing of the Edgar Laing building in lower Manhattan. Concurrently, Eiffel, an entrepreneurial engineer who dabbled in architecture, began to employ wrought iron in numerous buildings and façades around Paris, and Hector Guimard saw the potential of duplicating complex forms by casting multiples in iron. Yet, at the turn of the century, even the most adventurous architects would have been hard-pressed to execute their visions in technologically sophisticated form. Consider that the protean curves of Mendelsohn's Eisenstein Tower and the taut surfaces of Corbusier's Villa Savoye represent dramatically different architectural ideas yet share a common technology—a thin plaster skin troweled over a crude brick core.

If the modern era of technology in architecture had its roots in the first applications of cast iron, it went on to tensile materials, resins, and processes we know today. Most, if not all, were pioneered by other industries: vacuum-forming, rotational molding, spot welding, and high-performance coatings from the auto industry; metal spinning, blow-molding, fiberglass, extrusion, adhesive bonding, and molded plywood from aircraft. Fifty years ago George Nelson adopted World War II plastic "cocoon" technology to the production of translucent lamps and chairs that even today demonstrate a rare synthesis of design and production technology.

Today architects dream they will join the mainstream of production technology—that craft-based elements will be phased out of architecture, and that the agony of fabrication will someday take place in a digital kingdom where the click of a mouse will cause a machine to extrude, wrap, punch, and deliver what was once a recalcitrant hunk of iron ore, placing it exactly where the architect has decreed. But it is a long stride from "printing" a three-dimensional model to assembling a full-scale environment. The conjunction of design, tooling, fabrication, and assembly has never been more seductive, or for that matter more elusive, since while it is true that a common platform is now able, conceptually, to seamlessly leap from the mind to cyberspace to the punch press, and the crane, there has been no comparable reduction in the sheer mass and resistance of materials that make up the bulk of a building.

Looking back at the ropes, trestles, and levers once employed to lift heavy burdens, the gangs of men and livestock once required to power them, and the sole reliance on

Saarinen's work with General Motors in the 1950s exploited many of the automotive production techniques of which today's generation of designers are so enamored. The buildings are replete with die-cast ceiling systems and machined fittings, likely produced by GM's supply chain, which achieved an economic production run by replication throughout the entire complex. So the question confronting architects has to do with the contest between the custom-made and the off-the-shelf. Is the modularity that is implicit in mass production a corollary to the distribution/production complex, or will the unfolding world of five-axis mills, plasma-cutting, and rapid prototyping conjoin the heretofore exclusive realms of art and production technology?

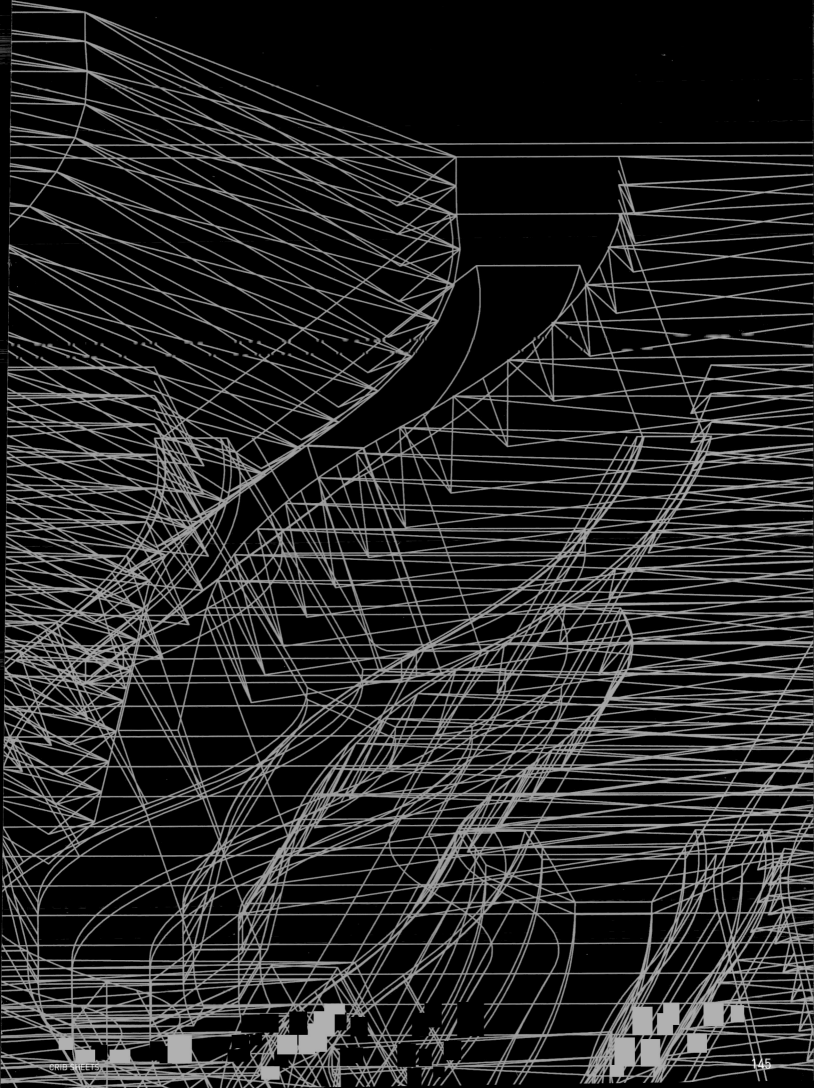

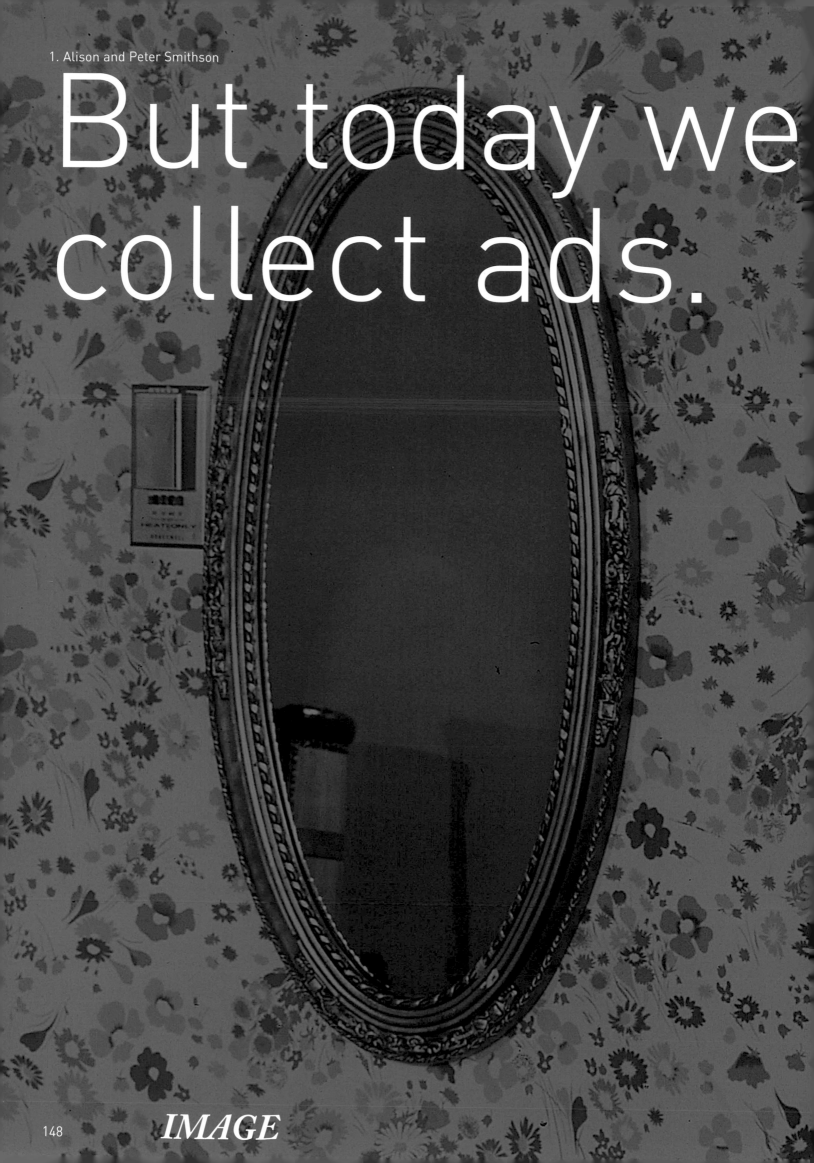

1. Alison and Peter Smithson

But today we collect ads.

IMAGE

2. Peter Eisenman
Media does better images than we do.

3. Ryue Nishizawa
Layered scenes appeared and disappeared like cells of animation.

4. Barry Katz
It was really during this period that a rigorous "philosophy of presentation" began to take shape within OSS.

5. Walter Benjamin
Architecture has always represented the prototype of a work of art the reception of which is consummated by a collectivity in a state of distraction.

6. Sergei M. Eisenstein
In themselves, the pictures, the phases, the elements of the whole are innocent and indecipherable. The blow is struck only when the elements are juxtaposed into a sequential image.

7. K. Michael Hays
This . . . is Mies's abstraction: the effort to turn subjective experience into objectivized form and images but that now flow back into the space of experience thus left open.

8. Charles Jencks
To those whose pursuit of the obsessive image is so complete and dedicated that one can say their pursuit of fashion is uncorruptible and of the highest integrity.

9. Bernard Tschumi
The purpose of the tripartite mode of notation (events, movements, spaces) . . . proceeds from a need to question the modes of representation generally used by architects: plans, sections, axonometrics, perspectives.

10. Kevin Lynch
This leads to the definition of what might be called *imageability*: that quality in a physical object which gives it a high probability of evoking a strong image in any given observer.

11. Deyan Sudjic
The buxom curves of the Coke bottle have made Coca-Cola not just a fizzy drink—"esteemed brain tonic" as it was called in its early days—but a universal symbol of Americana.

12. Hubert Damisch
Long before the invention of the airplane, men of art were able to obtain, largely through graphic means, "bird's-eye views," the image of the city being confound with its maquette, its relief plan.

13. Robert Venturi, Denise Scott Brown, Steven Izenour
This architecture of styles and signs is antispatial; it is an architecture of communication over space; communication dominates space as an element in the architecture and in the landscape. But it is for a new scale of landscape.

14. Paul Virilio
From the aesthetics of the appearance of stable images, present precisely because of their static nature, to the aesthetics of the disappearance of unstable images, present because of their motion (cinematic, cinemagraphic), a transmutation of representations has taken place.

15. Michael Sorkin
But the computer also provides another liberation. Secure in the knowledge that anything can be produced, drawing—sketching—is itself emboldened, offering a license that gives the sketch validity not simply as a source but as the final technical authority.

16. Jean Baudrillard
This would be the successive phases of the image:
—it is the reflection of a basic reality
—it masks and perverts a basic reality
—it masks the *absence* of a basic reality
—it bears no relation to any reality whatever:
  it is its own pure simulacrum.

17. Gilles Deleuze and Félix Guattari
Where there is close vision, space is not visual, or rather the eye itself has a haptic, nonoptical function: no line separates earth from sky, which are of the same substance; there is neither horizon nor background nor perspective nor limit nor outline or form nor center.

18. Jesse Reiser
The arguments that have been attached to media and its relation to architecture have generally focused on the information technologies associated with electronic or mass-media formations, hence the proliferation of projects by architects that attempt to recover for architectural space the fugitive and placeless condition inherent in electronic technologies.

19. Bernard Rudofsky
[The picture window's] popularity and growing use rest on the fact that it works both ways; it discloses to the passerby a glowing and carefully arranged picture of domesticity. Indeed, the wiseacres who poke fun at the occurrence of picture windows in those nightmarish "developments" of former potato fields into alleged towns, merely ignore their true function.

20. Herbert J. Gans
Actually, Levitt also used a highly variegated color scheme to increase diversity, so that only every 150th house was alike; besides, purchasers put their individual brand on the house and yard soon after they moved in. Their image of other houses was determined not by their façades, but by their occupants, so that (for neighbors at least) every house quickly became unique.

21. Beatriz Colomina
The state of distraction in the metropolis, described so eloquently by Walter Benjamin early in the twentieth century, seems to have been replaced by a new form of distraction, which is to say a new form of attention. Rather than wandering cinematically through the city, we now look in one direction and see many juxtaposed images, more than we can possibly synthesize or reduce to a single impression.

22. Johan Bettum
Where the image once allowed privileged access to the problems of composition and coded meaning, its present currency is framed by its capacity to register movement. For this purpose, the image is unique. In its expression of intensities, it allows relations to be mapped, keyed, and

23. Charles Jencks
Is the image of the Bauhaus in its building at Dessau or Weimar, in the Silver Prince Gropius or the Tough Prole Meyer, in its industrial design or in Habitat, with Johannes Itten or Moholy-Nagy? Has Image gone the way of brand and the American war on Iraq—a convenient mask to hide other things? Today cynicism holds the patent on these words, which is not to say they don't refer to important concepts.

24. Craig Hodgetts
Within a digital universe chock-full of competing images it is remarkable how little headway has been made by those that depict architecture. While its nice to see the latest cars and designer stuff parade past a significant building, and even nicer to enjoy a film (usually science-fiction) set in a pastiche of buildings-that-have-just-been-in-the-trades, the image of a building, at least in our culture, has long been established by its defining graphic presentation rather than its physical presence.

25. Sylvia Lavin
Although the image has received significant architectural attention in recent years, these discussions tend to deny the material dimension of visuality and to suppress the real labor of manufacturing the image. By undertaking the task of materializing the image through the surface, by concretizing the processes of image production and by intensifying the problematics of image consumption, Tschumi has used Le Fresnoy to give new force to the performative effects of architecture in the visible space of the real.

26. Jesse Reiser
We are less concerned with image than with communing with information directly—and indeed this is general to the "behavior" of architecture, which is largely unread, except by experts. The modality of reading architecture is made potent only when it is converted into representation, film, or a photograph. The critical theorists would insist upon our conscious decoding of architecture as representation, making an ethical necessity to be hyperconscious of image-reading as a way of unmasking perceived hidden "agendas" of power. A reactionary position would suggest that these agendas simply don't exist—indeed, they do. But we contend that architecture is a poor vehicle for handling these agendas—they must be addressed on the level of practice, not object.

27. Jason Payne

"Image" and its affiliated term "seeing" have increasingly limited use value in emerging architectural discourse. The term "seeing" tends toward the cerebral and the rational: "what you can think from what you see." But a new sensibility is emerging, one that's inevitable. It has more to do with sense, and sense implies matter. It's not what it is, but how it "feels." I say inevitable because you see this sensibility rising up everywhere, in unrelated disciplines—in contemporary theories of history, war, geopolitics, or engineering. Even rock music has shifted away from lyrical content, toward an increasing use of sound as substance. If we are to compete with these other disciplines in terms of cultural relevance then we must embrace this shifting sensibility.

28. Neil Denari

The term *image* commonly refers to subject matter or content (even when abstract), as in *imagery*. A more contemporary understanding of the image might be anything that is two dimensional, without body, without depth, a mere recording of something, as in photography, cinema, or television. This is essentially a definition of a medium, a technique that can produce images (McLuhan) and content is embedded in its intrinsic methodology of mechanical or electronic transference. As the painter Robert Ryman said: "There is never a question of what to paint, but only how to paint. The how of painting has always been the image, the end product." Since the 1960s we have been able to convincingly define images as something other than a technique.

29. Michael Bell

Afterimage is the operative term that I find in both Aldo Rossi's "memory" and in Greg Lynn's "movement-image." Both find their meaning in perception, if you rely on Henri Bergson's definition of afterimage, a time image, or a "movement image," as an intuited presence situated "between a thing itself" and its representation (matter and memory). While the image has a role in disseminating architecture, the time image and the afterimage are linked to themes of emergence and becoming. Bergson's *intuition* transcends the relativity of knowing something through translation or representation; intuition engenders a coincidence with the object and its movements. These themes need to be understood as linked to a wide range of urban subjects, each of which seek to understand as the space of the city from a private set of circumstances, but they remain in their infancy.

30. Diane Favro

An urban image reflects both the physical and the conceptual status of a specific city. Visitors to a city form an impression—a memory image—of what they have experienced based upon both the physical responses of their senses and the conceptual responses determined by culturally conditioned notions of what a city is, does, and means. But an urban image is not a pictorial representation, but the idea of the city produced in the minds of contemporary visitors. Each individual who passes through an urban environment devises a slightly different mental image, yet all visitors in any given period navigate the same physical and cultural terrain, together formulating a collective urban image that shares the same basic characteristics. Responsive to the physical environment, this image is highly visual in nature, yet is also forcefully shaped by such intangibles as urban "mood," character, and the sequencing of enriched experiences.

31. Aaron Betsky

Architecture is, as Mario Gandelsonas pointed out long ago, the only art that is both present and represents. The ability to produce an alternative and wholly new reality that is completely immersive separates architecture from other art forms, while at the same time the craft of building aspires to frame qualities that propose that alternative realities (art) come forward in a manner that allows us to concentrate on them. This creates difficulties not only for the status of architecture itself (is it art or structure?), but also for the exhibiting of architecture as art. Not only must it find ways of making itself clear in a manner alien to itself, in models, drawings, or photographs, but it must do so within the context of itself, a designed building such as a museum. To truly address this issue, architecture must represent itself in its own presence.

32. Helene Furján

The image today is becoming the brand-image, a format that threatens to absorb even the bastions of high art. Tied to the flows of capital and the circulation of goods, the logo reveals the hidden "agenda" of perhaps all images: marketing. Meanwhile, within today's streams of electronic and digitized data, the image's legibility and singularity is continuously eroding, and the increasing dissemination of images creates a distractive condition that might be termed *post-spectacular*. This diffusion is coupled with the distractive reception of urban terrains as posited by Walter Benjamin or Michel de Certeau, in which the image of the city is replaced by an *atmospheric condition*—a sensory milieu—and fluid seams of navigated but always fluctuating locations. The status of the image in architecture, and indeed the wider cultural context, has lost the (ocular-centric) dominance and legitimacy it built at least since the Renaissance, which enshrined it in the iconic photographs of the modernist era. Today the image has dissolved in its own flows and, like the

33. Alexandra Loew

Walter Benjamin observed that architecture is experienced in a state of distraction. It is the *image* that organizes the gaze, concentrates attention and produces desire, but where the photograph once buttressed architecture's weak frame, today this stability is confounded by new, contemporary desires. For Benjamin, the image—vis à vis the photograph—was the emblem of a culture that could be mass-produced; it consolidated those cultural changes put into effect by mechanical reproduction. Today legibility is less desirable, and a confluence of new technologies and sensibilities has replaced the camera and the vitrine with more virtual and suggestive apparatus.

Beatriz Colomina has argued that publicity is architecture's primary mode of existence: from glossy centerfolds to tomelike monographs, the image and its accompanying rhetoric remains architecture's most potent vehicle of dissemination. And yet, as the preoccupation with translucency and emergence short-circuits the unified front required to run a media campaign, the question becomes, is architecture undergoing an image crisis, or is it staging a publicity coup?

If architecture's pas de deux with image is to be re-choreographed, then to engage the suspension between real and virtual, reality and illusion, present conditions and future potentials, is where image and architecture rendezvous. Imageability reconciles these seemingly opposing forces. It condenses the diagram into a logo, neither indexing the process of its creation nor limiting its future possibilities. In this sense, image is operative—a modality that resists both the stability (image) and the legibility (index) of the frame and offers "intoxicating" distillation instead. Whereas midcentury imageability was a tool for producing a mental, ideological map of the city, a salve for urbanity's chaotic intensity, today's imageability gives us a vision for something that is as yet unseen.

Architecture remains the privileged domain of the scopophiliac, but the discrete frame or a linear processional has given way to the intricacies, networks, and swarms of more supple organizations. Once the space between the mental map and the afterimage has been forced open to include potentials not yet visualized, image is but a flutter in things that coalesce in fleeting and serial moments. Trajectories preside over iconography; atmospheric distraction is preferable to concentrated attention. After all, an image that is too "hot" or transparent leaves little to the imagination and to the production of desire. For the same reasons, image is no longer desirable as a tool for framing and stabilizing, because "fixed" and "stable" are no longer useful ways of conceptualizing the world. "What you see is what you get" gives way to "You ain't seen nothing yet."

Nip/tuck

1. Alejandro Zaera-Polo

Operation: A controlled manipulation or exchange with an intended performance.

2. Hashim Sarkis

Today mats are appearing everywhere. We call them fields, grounds, carpets, matrices.

3. Richard Neutra

Forms around us became dictated by an industrial technology and justified by "operation."

4. Rem Koolhaas

To be operational today, you have to abstain from large claims, including being operational.

5. Sheila Kennedy

Structure and ornament merge in the play of materials as the categories of the aesthetic and the operative coincide.

6. MVRDV

One way to study the world of numbers is through the use of "extremizing scenarios." They lead to frontiers, edges, and therefore to inventions.

7. Greg Lynn

One doesn't have to mindlessly use the "new paradigm," but I think architects do have a responsibility to critically reflect on whatever that paradigm is.

8. Michael Speaks

As networks become more powerful, competition among cities will no longer be for market share but for affiliative links that add value through the introduction of difference.

9. Michel de Certeau

These operations—multiform and fragmentary, relative to situations and details, insinuated into and concealed within devices whose mode of usage they constitute, and thus lacking their own ideologies or institutions.

10. Michel Foucault

Nowadays arrangement has taken over from extension, which had once replaced localization. It is defined by relationships of neighborhood between points and elements, which can be described formally as series, trees, and networks.

11. Charles Jencks

Ideas and forms are stolen from fashion, movies, comic books, deep-sea diving, space exploration, technology, biology, robotology . . . Anything is acceptable so long as it is slightly interesting, different from the present and exotic.

12. Stan Allen

Lifescape is a design strategy that recognizes humanity as a symbiotically evolving, globally interconnected, and technologically enhanced system . . . It is fully integrative. Lifescape is not a loose metaphor or representation—it is a functioning reality, an autopoetic agent.

13. Sulan Kolatan

Lumping: Combining initially unrelated elements or structures; constructing lateral connections between categories.

Tuning: Adjusting within an extreme range of variation.

Co-citation: Indexing relatedness between unrelated cases, classes or fields.

Scaling: Testing a particular spatial logic at different scales.

14. Alex Wall

Operationally, if not experientially, the infrastructures and flows of material have become more significant than static political and spatial boundaries . . . The emphasis shifts from *forms* of urban space to *processes* of urbanization, processes that network across vast regional—if not global—surfaces.

15. Sanford Kwinter

A form arises from something called a *déploiement universel* ("universal unfolding"), a dynamical pathway in which every virtuality is activated, even though only some get chosen. Forms are always new and unpredictable unfoldings shaped by their adventures in time.

16. Bruce Mau
Bowie staged his identity in exaggerated scale to the point where each new staging ceased to feel new. Madonna, however, continues to pull herself constantly out of the background; indeed, her gestures are so effective that she convinces us that this act of reinvention is what life's all about.

17. Johan Bettum
An operation presupposes a subject, something that quietly disappeared from architecture as an extrinsic entity in the German *Späthistorismus* of the late nineteenth century. Nowadays the only subject that remains for architecture to operate upon is architecture itself, a fact that requires a good amount of self-irony, methodological precision, and the greatest discipline.

18. Craig Hodgetts
Although the first wave of industrialization seemed to reduce the architect's choices to the singular operation of assembly, the evolution of industrial processes from the linear Victorian organization to flexible computer-driven systems has enabled research and design to achieve a theoretically seamless relationship between input, concept, design, production, and marketing.

19. Michael Weinstock
[Emergence] is a word that is increasingly common in architectural discourse, where too often it is used to conjure complexity but without the attendant concepts and mathematical instruments of science . . . The task for architecture is to delineate a working concept of emergence and to outline the mathematics and processes that can make it useful to us as designers.

20. Sylvia Lavin
Rejecting the question of the proper (or even improper) relation between architectural subjects and objects might permit a new emphasis on interobjective questions such as, "What is the effect of this architectural object in the world of other objects?" Criticism might lose interest in "How does it make me feel?" and develop strategies for considering "What does it do?"

21. Servo
The museum exhibition has become an important terrain for contemporary architectural practice-as-research. No longer can work remain on paper, "speculating" on the future of technology or possible urban scenarios—the exhibition requires aggressive speculation of what is possible now, pushing at the boundaries of various discursive and representational quandaries, and turning the gallery into a space for built research.

22. Mark Goulthorpe
Greg Lynn suggested . . . that using animation software could create form that would move people in new ways by creating an impulsion, a peripheral movement. He looked to deriving geological rather than geographical form, to implicate force-in-form, which was an incredibly bold initiative. The provocation was that a new technological tool would allow a completely revised cultural and material potential for architecture.

23. Jesse Reiser
There is an example of operative practice that relates to metalworking: when you temper a blade, you're watching a rainbow of oxidation moving along a piece of metal and tracking that movement, which is a sign of a certain reaction in the crystal structure. This effect was known before science quantified it, people discovered it as a material practice. We are tracking the same kind of developments in architectural design and using it very precisely. This is a form of semiotics, but one that is not about representation.

24. Michael Bell
Transformation was the key term in Peter Eisenman's structuralist work in the 1970s. In the 1990s the term *operation* became prominent, though its origin is not as easy to locate or demonstrate. I continually find myself referring to an early passage in Gilles Delueze's *The Fold* that suggests that it's not "objects" but "objectiles" that should interest us. The term *operation* has always seemed a stand-in or heuristic term to me: it is not linked to emergent themes or to transformation, but it does indicate an unfolding and a becoming, and, like transformation, it relieves the author of apparent intent.

25. Greg Lynn
At the moment architecture was able to generate its own theoretical armature, discriminate its own "zeitgeist" and formulate its own arguments, when it had a very clear understanding of a contemporary architectural project (with the work of Aldo Rossi, for example) is exactly when it was the most boring, the most unattended to by culture. Now is a time when architecture is particularly "hot" with practitioners of other fields—musicians, artists, museum curators, fashion designers, automobile designers, follow our field more meticulously than others. But at the same time, it is also a moment in which we're curiously least able to formulate our own discourse within the academy.

OPERATION

26. Manuel de Landa

To be able to apply the genetic algorithm at all, a particular field of art needs to first solve the problem of how to represent the final product (a painting, a song, a building) in terms of the process that generated it, and then, how to represent this process itself as a well-defined sequence of operations. It this sequence, or rather, the computer code that specifies it, that becomes the "genetic material" of the painting, song, or building in question . . . *architects wishing to use this new tool must not only become hackers* (so that they can create the code needed to bring extensive and intensive aspects together) *but also be able "to hack" biology, thermodynamics, mathematics, and other areas of science to tap into the necessary resources.*

27. Marc Angélil and Sarah Graham

Operation-Urbanity: how would understandings of urban structure develop when exposed to the changes brought about by operational processes? Tracing forces at work in the formation of urban territories, understanding the city as a dynamic system, addresses architecture's formal condition not as a license for the use of a-priori determined form but as a circumstance evolving from production. Searching for strategies predicated on interactive and varying means of adaptation (how are the morphogenetic processes of urban assemblages conceived?), a discourse is opened on the relation between genesis and form, between operative procedures and urban organization. Form materializes through processes of translation and transformation. Varying parameters act upon one another to chart a differential field within which development takes place, contributing at each stage of the process to the crystallization of formal constructs.

28. Steven Johnson

On the screen, the pixels dance: bright red dots with faint trails of green, scurrying across a black background, like fireflies set against the sky of a summer night. For a few seconds, the movement on-screen looks utterly random: pixels darting back and forth, colliding, and moving on. And then suddenly a small pocket of red dots gather together in a pulsing, erratic circle, ringed by a strip of green. The circle grows as more red pixels collide with it; the green belt expands. Seconds later, another lopsided circle appears in the corner of the screen, followed by three more. The circles are unlike any geometric shape you've ever seen. They seem more like a life-form—a digital blob—pulsing haphazardly, swelling and contracting. Two blobs slowly creep toward each other, then merge, forming a single unit.

29. Alejandro Zaera-Polo

Processes are far more interesting than ideas, which are linked to existing codes, operating critically or in alignment with other, preexisting, systems of ideas. Rather than turning a project into the implementation of an idea or the scaffolding for an image, we are interested in constructing differing engineering-based processes. If geological, biological, or social histories have something to teach us, for instance, it is that these processes of temporal formation produce organizations of far greater complexity and sophistication than instantaneous ideas or visions. This is perhaps the most important development brought about by information technology to our practice: we can design, synthesize, and proliferate specific histories and scripts for a project. In this way, a project becomes the construction of a microhistory, a kind of specific construction narrative. The essence of the project is formed in a sequence where additional complexity is constructed to integrate incoming information.

We are no longer trapped within the traditional compulsion to reproduce historical models, or to invent new models from scratch. We do not have to produce a project as a reproduction, a derivation, or the invention of a historical model. We do not need to produce complexity by making collages. We can synthesize the historical processes in a kind of accelerated motion, integrally adding information to the assemblage.

30. R. E. Somol

Instrumental. Performative. Infrastructural. Operational. Projective. Increasingly impatient with the representational preoccupations of postmodernism and deconstruction (not to mention the narrative theme creation of commercial environments), segments within contemporary architecture have assumed positions associated with the above set of terms as a way to move beyond an analysis (or hermeneutics) revolving around "what architecture means" toward an experimentation (or heuretics) engaged with "what architecture can do." This operational cadre has had to confront a fifty-year history that has emphasized the rhetorical possibilities of architecture, registered through increasingly mannered or extreme form, which can be said to have been initiated by the pedagogies developed at the University of Texas at Austin in the mid-1950s. The techniques and priorities associated with this attempt to advance a self-reflective language of modern architecture has underwritten a design agenda that values criticality (if sometimes only achieving the ironic) and difficulty (if often settling for the merely complicated). While the Austin pedagogy (and, subsequently, those of Cornell, Cooper Union, and the ETH) aimed to formalize space or make it figurative, the operational paradigm, which may have first emerged among a particular coterie within the Architectural Association in the early 1970s, insists on dynamizing space, exposing and releasing the forces that provisionally give shape to time. While the spatial fixation of the Austin legacy first requires "seeing" space (e.g., through the gestalt effect of figure/ground reversal) and the subsequent generation of retinal objects, the AA model wagers on material processes. The earlier optical regime has been exchanged for a thermodynamic orientation.

If the central identifying trait of the architectural discipline for the optical-mathematic legacy of Texas was geometry, then the reciprocal defining characteristic for the dynamic-material regime of the AA is power. And, indeed, it is largely this shift from geometry to power (and, by extension, from the drawing to the diagram) that has allowed architectural practice and pedagogy to move away from their longstanding representational obsessions toward the operational or performative. This is not to suggest that the geometric project of architecture has disappeared, as it has regained a second life in some international circles by exactly attaching itself to the concerns of mobility, at least that form of mobility as offered by digital animation. But a fuller investigation of architecture's use of and by power, its capacity to instigate alternative lifestyles and new forms of collective organization, requires it to disentangle itself from its fascination with geometry. Inspired by Michel Foucault's writings on the panopticon and heterotopias, the operational attitude has manifested itself through an attention to the organizational effects evidenced at the AA, for example, by Robin Evan's work on prisons as well as the shift from the matrix to the corridor plan: Bernard Tschumi's experiments with cross-programming, and Rem Koolhaas's celebration of the behavioral possibilities enabled by the skyscraper stack combined with the elevator as its expedient device for multiplying virtual "plots" or scenarios. The operational school emphasizes how architectural plans engender or instigate social and political effects, and experiments with alternative models for how new social lives could be imagined: what is the diagram for organizing bodies and behaviors, how can this world be projected, what are its forms of conjugality?

This line of inquiry might reveal that extreme forms do not necessarily entail or produce new styles of living, and that such new lifestyles (now no longer reducible to a consumer category) do not always require convoluted, exceptional forms. Moreover, while exceptional form may be requisite for a critical practice (which is recognized on the representational register), they might well be redundant (if not counterproductive) for a projective one, which is organized at the operational level. Here, the operation (as technical procedures or steps) and the operational (as mode of projection) might be usefully distinguished. Operations tend to provide automatic means to suggest complicated (intricate) depth. This has always been the insight of the "process" school of resistant legibility, of which Peter Eisenman is the undisputed godfather. In contrast, the pursuit of the operational may require a concerted effort, but its effects are evanescent (or potentially invisible), and this is the trajectory of what might be called the *parti* school of organizational infrastructure: potentially hard work that looks easy (when it doesn't disappear entirely). The bias of critical operations is additive and intricate: layering, superposition, collage, montage, folding, and so on. The tendency of the operational is toward reduction and expediency: erasure, voiding, condensation, distillation. In recent history, the academy has been much better at teaching the former, which is connected to an elaborate system of process, precedent, and critical evaluation. Today, of course, operations have become the default of digital technologies, as means now serve as their own ends. For the operational, however, means are only useful for a particular end, and the value and significance of such ends must continuously be negotiated, argued, and asserted. This choice between operations (as procedures) and the operational (as projective) can be finally associated with two current agendas in academic research and design: the school of technique, and the school of polemic.

OPERATION

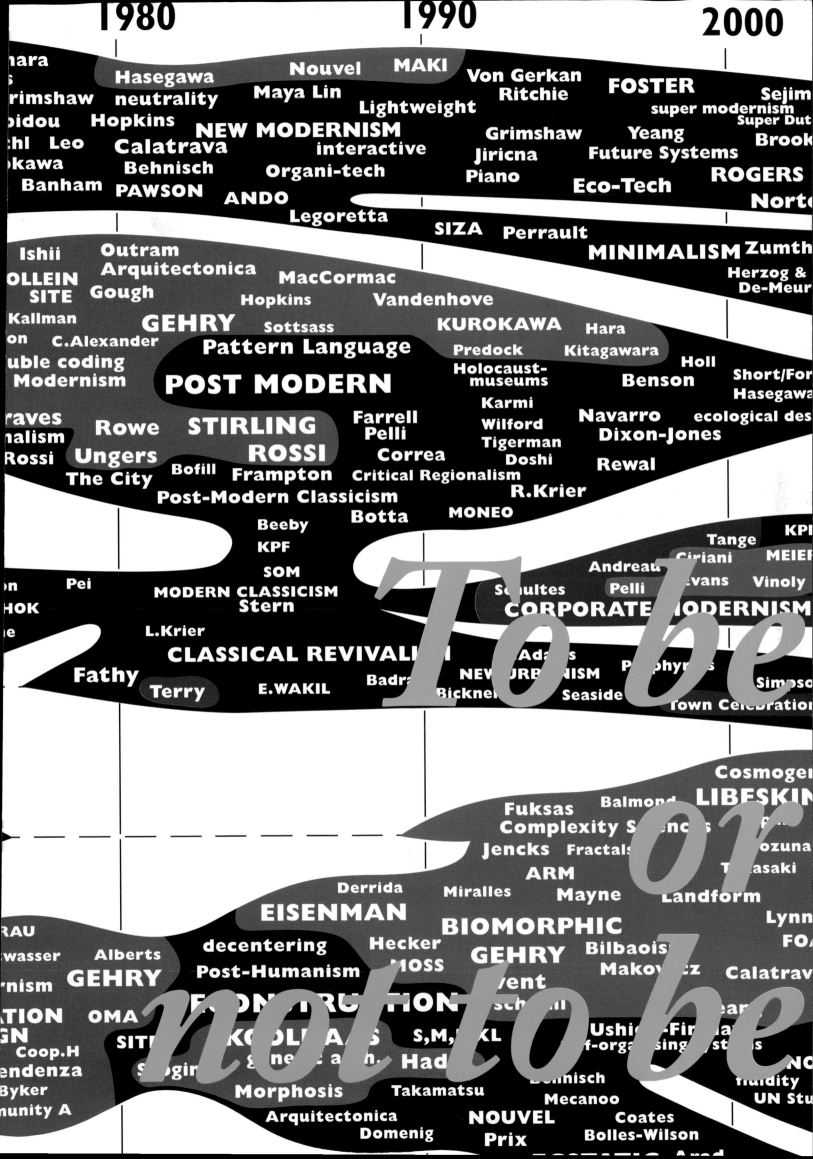

Sometimes a cigar is just a cigar.

CRITICALITY

2. Antonio Gramsci
Pessimism of the intellect, optimism of the will.

3. Peter Eisenman
The critical becomes generative as opposed to being reactive or resistant.

4. Greg Lynn
Every creative practice relies on the introduction of a critical innovation that transforms the discipline in some way.

5. Michael Speaks
There are more creative alternatives to dealing with the often deadening sameness of commercial culture than resistance or complicity.

6. Herbert Muschamp
For me, criticism is about crisis. Being a critic means to call things into crisis, and there's always a new crisis.

7. Jean Baudrillard
We are no longer a part of the drama of alienation; we live in the ecstasy of communication. And this ecstasy is obscene.

8. Alejandro Zaera-Polo
Criticality is an ingredient to be deployed with enormous discretion in a production; if it becomes too obvious, it spoils the taste of the materials.

9. Gregory Ulmer
There is a certain equivalence in "false criticism," in any case, between dreamwork and analysis, promising that inventions may be *written*—generated—without having to be "thought" first.

11. Craig Hodgetts
As a compass, capable of directing resources, challenging preconceptions, and motivating experimentation, the position of critical theory as a partner in the creative process has never been more effective (or more important).

12. Sanford Kwinter
It is a fundamentally bourgeois idea to live the "critical" life, to assess the value of objects and practices when the processes of production are themselves wild and alive and doing their business semi-independently elsewhere.

13. Peter Eisenman
It is not a question of what architecture should mean, but whether architecture should mean at all . . . It is at this moment that the idea of an architecture of the post-critical enters, and offers itself as an alternative.

14. Surrealist Manifesto
We declare as follows to the entire braying literary, dramatic, philosophical, exegetical and even theological body of contemporary criticism . . . we intend to show the fragility of thought, and on what shifting foundations, what caverns we have built our trembling houses.

15. R. E. Somol
Criticality exists by producing legibility and distancing effects. Both are linked to an intellectual problem of the 1960s and 1970s that is no longer viable. Through its own success, the critical project has reached its condition of limitation. The returns are no longer worth the investment.

16. Johan Bettum
The architectural object can hardly be held

17. Greg Lynn

The rebuilding of the World Trade Center towers might best be done by an architect who does not specialize in towers, because there needs to be some critical reflection on their design and construction to adequately respond to the event. There needs to be an oblique critical gesture that is commensurate with the cultural and political significance of the site.

18. Russell Fortmeyer

Broad terms, like *postmodernism* and *criticality*, can mean almost anything and that's why they aren't too useful. However, criticality does suggest a self-awareness—an understanding of the discipline of architecture. Criticality is the "minority view" in architecture—the research engine of the discipline, the modus operandi for dispersing a new set of stylistic tricks into the mainstream. Discussion of a critical project lasts only until it reemerges as something new.

19. Manfredo Tafuri

Criticism as one of the dimensions of architectural activity, has to satisfy two basic conditions:
A. It has to renounce systematic expression in favor of a compromise with daily contingencies. Its model should be journalistic extravaganza rather than the definitive essay which is complete in itself.
B. The critical *field* will have to adjust its scale: from the analysis of the architectural *object* to the criticism of the global contexts that condition its configuration.

20. K. Michael Hays

There is now a vaster de-differentiation of disciplines and the tendentious erasure of boundaries between specific cultural materials and practices, that have homogenized all distinction, difference, and otherness into a globalized, neutralized sameness. Much of what claims to be progressive postcritical thought is happy to aestheticize this situation, promote its effects, and trade in any remaining individuality or singularity of thought or practice for a randomized, spread out delirium. But even for us remaining critical theorists, "critique"... is an ambivalent concept now.

21. Sulan Kolatan

The argument that criticality is a question of distance does not necessarily hold anymore. There are prominent instances, particularly in popular cultural domains such as film and music, where critical work becomes simultaneously embraced by mainstream culture. The field of architecture has such cases, too, albeit to a lesser degree. What these kinds of works share is the capacity to operate and communicate on a number of levels substantial and superficial elements developing a productive relationship with one another in order to enhance rather than weaken the overall effect.

22. Mark Mack

Theory is of no "use" to architecture anymore. Good architects need no theory per se; Gehry, Holl, Himmelblau, and Murcutt create exciting, thought-provoking architecture without the divisive and speculative prose of theorizing. Bad architects like Eisenman, Libeskind, and Koolhaas need their theorists, who praise their masters like minstrels in a medieval court. These theorists are not interpreting a culture but using the architect's work to channel them into curated shows, managing, in the process, to become "gatekeepers" of cultural and architectural institutions. No such intellectual questioning of our culture, values, or ambitions can take place anymore.

23. Jeffrey Kipnis

Having thoroughly migrated to, percolated through and reconfigured most of the existing niches in the ecology of self-consciousness, criticality has now stalled—for the moment at least—as a creative eruption. Compelled to move with nowhere else to go, criticality transmogrifies into a social hegemony, an etiquette of doing and talking that is less productive than courtly, less thoughtful than mean. In this frustrated humor, criticality suppresses other moments, other moods, livelier ones, giddier ones, ones wetter, more freshly, more rhythmic, more transporting, more creative and much more intelligent. Its potency ossifies into a regime of manners, a sadistic stultification that, like a vampire, eroticizes the bloodless ennui it engenders, an ennui that continues to pose as sobriety, as depth, but is now merely the ache of unrealized potential.

24. Aaron Betsky

Criticism comes from outside and breaks open the "closed box" of the building, creating an opening within the efficient production of architecture and its smooth consumption. The norm for construction shifts from producing the maximum amount of square feet that can be optimally used for the least amount of money, resources, and energy, to include "opening something up" in the process of construction itself that allows us to realize the true value of what has been made. This surplus is by its very nature always in dispute, because every definition and interpretation will be different. The critic has, as her or his task, the finding of such moments of inconsistency, too much or not quite yet, that open up this possibility of miss-using construction. Criticism is the enemy of value engineering.

CRITICALITY

25. Michael Bell

The role of the *critical* work of architecture has migrated to wide-ranging studies made of the economic or infrastructural nature of the "contemporary city." From MVRDV to the Harvard Project on the City to a wide array of urban recovery/description projects such as Thom Mayne's LA Now or my own work on housing policy, criticality has been slightly delayed or suspended while a new model of the city is drawn. For me, MVRDV's datascapes or the statistical modeling of the Harvard Project on the City are not an end themselves—or even something to receive or rebut criticism—but a reconnaissance project to understand where, when, and how one might again be "critical" or develop an architecture capable of being this kind of in face of immense systems of production. The era of this kind of architecture is potentially given new life here as it finds new footing and as these architects verge on joining the production systems themselves.

26. Jesse Reiser

Compared to politics, architecture is fundamentally a material practice, and the final lasting effects of architecture are material, not practical. There has been a misplaced anthropomorphism projected on architecture that is basically metaphysical—even superstitious—which ascribes to architecture the human traits of choice and volition.

A modality of criticality that sees danger in everything and everyone bases its forces on *prohibition*. There is another affirmative modality of the critical that occurs as a by-product of radical invention. It is nonmetaphorical, nonfundamental, and disinterested in the origins or being of things. Rather, its critical function consists of the loosening and expansion of received categories and orders. It is the transformation of once-stable and discrete models of architecture that offers the most promise for an expansion of architectural effects. Indeed the critical dimension of this direction of work lies in the capacity to extend and free up historically determined models, to harness the almost limitless productivity of material flows.

27. Charles Jencks

Criticality, a term developed in the recent sciences of complexity, concerns the way all systems reach a "critical" stage when pushed far from equilibrium. The first proof of this universal principle was with the scientist Per Bak's sand pile experiments, a quasi-architectural test. Sand-added to a pyramidal structure (just as Egyptian architects built steeper than the critical angle for pyramids) resulted in landslides at all scales. This demonstrated that all self-organizing systems (embryonic and population growth, the stock market) might tend toward this point and lead to unpredictable, sudden change. "Self-organizing criticality" is now a leading science, which doesn't mean architects pay it much attention.

Architects such as Peter Eisenman and critics such as Robert Somol and Jeff Kipnis argue for "the critical" as a creative critical investigation of the conditions of architecture—its language in Eisenman's case, and a dialectical criticism of what exists, or a resistance to the status quo, in the critics' case. "Critical theory" became a mantra for academics in the early 1980s, especially those looking for tenure, but the presuppositions underlying so much of it—particularly those of the Frankfurt School—were accepted *uncritically*. (Which doesn't mean it was wrong.)

My concept of Critical Modernism, developed in the late 1990s, argues for a hidden tradition of modernism that is critical both of previous modernisms, and the condition of culture and the environment as it finds them. Thus, the dialectic of opposing positions, thus, the sixty or so movements that are countermovements, thus, the internal debate within the profession and engagement with social issues outside it. Critical Modernism is transhistorical, in the sense that no single architect or group or style or set of attitudes encompasses its goals. Nevertheless, certain architects and critics may be consciously involved with this larger project, and the dynamic morality behind the motives explains the inversions, the fact that there are modern movements in the plural.

28. Sylvia Lavin

Once upon a time there was criticism. It was a lovely way of writing, full of wit, intelligence, and cunning. But slowly, its promise was distorted: formalists made it narrow, phenomenologists made it precious, and operatives made it covert. History and theory came to criticism's rescue, discrediting dangerous forms of essentialisms, shining bright light on blind spots and airing out "closets" made fetid by secret ambitions. Although at first they fought over who had the better cure, history and theory ultimately joined forces to give criticism a strong dose of critical resistance to what they feared as the most horrible enemy of all: commodification. Sadly, as so often happens, the cure was worse than the disease and resistance disfigured the once-charming genre until it was so mangled by criticality that criticism nearly died.

Yet, this mishap was recent enough that it is still possible to selectively harvest critical organs and use them not to resist but to awaken a new criticism. Criticism's innocence will never be reborn, however, criticism is not condemned to a Frankenstein-like existence, forever ill at ease and forsaken in a world that doesn't understand its value. Contemporary criticism will, to the contrary, appear deceptively comfortable in today's world, with a swagger that only comes from a good credit rating. It will use the lessons learned by the theoretical and historical work of the past thirty years to clear itself from bankruptcy and become a valuable commodity of contemporary culture.

Manfredo Tafuri holds the key to this exchange, for he did the most to discredit and ultimately bankrupt criticism. Like most good members of the party, Tafuri didn't actually give his resources away to the poor. Instead, after defining criticism as a concern of current architecture, he stopped writing about new design. But while some took this as a sign that contemporary architecture was both a forbidden and useless subject, Tafuri became a repo man, hoarding criticism's valuable and uncanny ability to appreciate newness, burying it deeper and deeper in texts hermetically sealed by intentionally repellent language. Arguing that everything new is just the most recent old thing, Tafuri receded not into history but hid behind oldness, where he maintained more than his honor; he kept the very idea of newness safe from what he thought were the perils of design culture.

These days, if you try to hide in the oldness of Venice, the subject of Tafuri's late work, you are more likely to rub elbows with Indiana Jones than you are with moral rectitude. Criticality was needed once upon a time to serve as a prophylaxis that separated the intellectual and the architect from the contamination of a capitalized professional, but resistance is now futile. Instead, the gap Tafuri used as a protective barrier has itself become a covert operative that merely isolates writing from design. No matter how many hybrid architect/writers do both, resistant criticality still inflicts on writing the duty to make everything "old" and "forever," while condemning design to be the automatic and thoughtless agent of newness.

Having been inoculated against the many serious diseases that ailed criticism, writing can be confident that it now has adequate antibodies stored up to confront newness. In fact, criticism can thank Tafuri for using criticality to allow writing to promote and even produce newness as a closely guarded secret. Rested and rejuvenated, no longer suspicious of newness nor feeling dependent on design to confer it, criticism can now be attentive to writing itself, using its pleasures to create new objects of study and claiming new effects for scholarship and intellection. New criticism will capitalize on its engagement with commodity culture to make history and theory contemporary and to give architecture more value, not less. During the past thirty years, despite Tafuri's valiant efforts to slip critical resistance into history, oldness made much more money than newness. But those Venetian ducals—real gold coins that are old and heavy yet offer no resistance to the virtual forms of capital that could constitute new resources for criticism—can't buy the "bling" that makes being rich a pleasure today.

Long, long ago, when criticism was young, it was the language of beauty and pleasure. Philosophy, jealous of criticism's allure, and fearful of the lapses in decorum criticism's quixotic appeal often caused, discredited its fulsome rhetoric and tried to put the stabilizing prose of analytic aesthetics in its place. But the substitution ultimately failed, because criticism was not merely about pleasure but was itself a pleasure. In this promiscuous isomorphism between writer and object, an intimacy feared not only by philosophy but even more so by criticality, lay powerful reinforcements, tactical agility, and the momentary usefulness of being able to bring new forms of pleasure into being. For now, criticism offers an especially appealing means of evoking newness and today's particular pleasures, those that ought not only to be staked out as historically and theoretically legitimate concerns of architectural discourse but have been urgently claimed as the most coveted of all architectural qualities.

COMMUNITY

Privatopia

Belluschi

Yamasaki

MEGAPOLIS

Utzon

Lewerentz

Kikuta

Dominion

Albini

LINCO

Aulenti

A.ALTO

Johansen

Greene

Neo-Liberty

G.Bohm

SCHAROUN

Erskine

NEO-EXPRESSI

Goff

Keisler

Niemeyer

Dolce

Michelucci

T Ronchamp

Blow-up

Fantaztic

plug in

POP

Hausserman

Johansen

ARCHIGRAM

Kurokawa

sqiatters

METABOLISM

UTOPI

Price

situatic

Student-Act

Jacobs

Dro

COMMUNITY

2. West Side Story
Skyscrapers bloom in America

3. Charles Baudelaire
Il faut épater le bourgeois.

4. Edward J. Blakely and Mary Gail Snyder
The American middle class is forting up.

5. Alejandro Zaera-Polo
Community is a zone of consistent traits in the texture of a population.

6. Tom Wolfe
The battle to be the least bourgeois of all became somewhat loony.

7. Russell Fortmeyer
A community is an unplanned collection of individuals with at least one common aim.

8. Craig Gore
But these places were so secure I couldn't, for the f---ing life of me, get into one. I finally had to pay a security guard on the gate $300 to look the other way.

9. Marc Augé
The space of non-place creates neither singular identity nor relations; only solitude, and similitude . . . The non-place is the opposite of utopia: it exists, and it does not contain any organic society.

10. Mark Landesbaum and Heidi Evans
Mission Viejo—swim capital of the world, mecca for medalists, home of the perfect-10 high dive, three competition swimming pools but only one public library—is nestled alongside a freeway in the rolling hills of south Orange County.

11. Sylvia Lavin
Architecture's use of sociological imagery, like happy children at school or battered women in shelters or even the more abstract image of crowds in motion, tends to overestimate its truth-value and underestimate its value in establishing standards of good behavior.

12. Rem Koolhaas
The Club represents the complete conquest— floor by floor—of the Skyscraper by social activity . . . In the Downtown Athletic Club the Skyscraper is used as a Constructivist Social Condenser: a machine to generate and intensify desirable forms of human intercourse.

13. Bernard Rudofksy
The picture window seldom affords a view of anything more picturesque than the picture window of one's neighbor. Its popularity and growing use rest on the fact that it works both ways: it discloses to the passer-by a glowing and carefully arranged picture of domesticity.

14. Marshall Berman
Ten minutes on this road, an ordeal for anyone, is especially dreadful for people who remember the Bronx as it used to be, who remember these neighborhoods as they once lived and thrived, until this road itself cut through their heart and made the Bronx, above all, a place to get out of.

15. Mike Davis
The carefully manicured lawns of Los Angeles's Westside sprout forests of ominous little signs warning: "Armed Response!" Even richer neighborhoods in the canyons and hillsides isolate themselves behind walls guarded by gun-toting private police and state-of-the-art electronic surveillance.

16. Doorn Manifesto
Urbanism considered and developed in terms of the Charte d'Athènes tends to produce "towns" in which vital human associations are inadequately expressed. To comprehend these human associations we must consider every community as a particular *total* complex. In order to make this *comprehension* possible, we propose to study urbanism as communities of varying degrees of complexity.

17. J. G. Ballard

Town-scapes are changing. The open-plan city belongs to the past—no more *ramblas*, no more pedestrian precincts, no more left banks and Latin quarters. We're moving into the age of security grilles and defensible space. As for living, our surveillance cameras can do that for us. People are locking their doors and switching off their nervous systems.

18. Michael Bell

At its best, "community" signifies a self-organizing system and a self-determining, volatile kind of negotiation. The term's emergence and near-ubiquitous use in urban redevelopment signals many people's unhappiness with the anonymity or autonomy of the techniques that produce most cities today. The term is easy to find fault with and is just as often invoked as a means to stall development rather than enliven it. Nevertheless, its roots are important and the emotions it reveals are meaningful.

19. Lynn Spigel

The central preoccupation of the new suburban culture was the construction of a particular *discursive space* through which the family could mediate the contradictory impulses for a private haven on the one hand, and community participation on the other. By lining up individual housing units on connecting plots of land, the suburban tract was itself the ideal articulation of this discursive space; the dual goals of separation from and integration into the larger community was the basis of tract design.

20. Michael Speaks

Clusters reveal today a veritable fractal structure in which similar lifestyle groups may be of different races, classes, genders, and live in geographically distinct regions of the city, state or country. No cultural monoculture, the United States is a nested, super-ecology of networks and clusters that rub against each other but which overlap in the nodal points of what used to be called the city . . . Clusters, or lifestyles, are identity-in-transit, and herald the emergence of post-market, commercial network communities on an unprecedented scale.

21. Craig Hodgetts

"Community" is an elastic entity composed of those individuals who express interest in a subject. Thus, a community may consist of anything from a very few individuals spread throughout the world, who may in fact never see one another face to face, to a very large group who are concentrated in a single space. Designation of a community is often conferred by an outside observer, oblivious to the actual participants. In architecture, then, the identification of those whose interests form conjunctive points within a specific project is often a primary determinant of a project's ultimate destiny.

22. Greg Lynn

To experiment, you don't need patrons, a museum, or a Prada. Indeed, it may be that the official patronage avenues for architecture are the most difficult places in which to do experimental work. If there's anywhere that experimentation is going to be permitted, it's alternative housing, immigrants' churches, children's day-care facilities, hospices, schools, and public housing, not only because they do not have a "taste" culture dictating design, but also because these groups need an identity that has not yet evolved. Experimentation and innovation are part of the design task.

23. Jesse Reiser

Traditional regionalism, like any fundamentalism, is the true international style. Regionalism is more homogenous, structurally, than globalism, as all regionalisms are structurally the same—only the semantic narrative of their local inflection differs. "Regionalism" is a reactionary concept, which only became visible when it began to die. There is another affirmative notion of the regional that is fundamentally artificial. This understanding assumes that new regionalisms can be created. "Neoregionalism" would in fact be a kind of new globalization, in which the regional emerges out of, and is immanent to, the global, rather than the other way around.

24. Charles Jencks

Artificial, temporary, and traditional communities all overlap and compete today. Aldo van Eyck posed the problem: "If society has no form, can architects design the counter-form?" Voluntaristic communities—associations, Web sites, professional bodies, interest groups of all kinds—tend to be nonlocal and therefore find no architectural expression. By contrast, traditional communities, in competition with the fast-changing associations, tend to be eroded and stifling. Everyone wants communities to exist except the ones they hate. When an architect or politician invokes "community," ask if it is based on place, or rather the root word "communication," two very different kinds of association.

25. Mark Mack

We have just exited the twentieth century, the most violent in history, with more people killed in wars than ever before, and this new century doesn't look much more promising. Soon, we'll all be living under a stringent democratic dictatorship where, due to patriotic angst, readiness to defend or attack is paramount and the distinction between civil and military interests become almost invisible. Like people awakened by a bad dream, architects, more than ever, need a call to conscience, need to stop dreaming about which form is weak or strong, which shape is cool and sexy—we need to insert some consciousness back into our profession.

26. Dora Jones

In addition to, and often in contrast with, an affection for technology, architecture in the twentieth century was deeply devoted to the well-being of man. Before World War II, technological innovation promised a sociocultural revolution, epitomized in architecture by the proletarian "machine for living." As ideologies grew more complex during and after World War II, architecture's revolutionary role became similarly more protracted—taking on the task of amelioration as an applied science. From the psychologizing of interiors to the anthropology of spatial practices in city planning, design came to be imagined as a solution to ills at every level of society. It was thought that good houses would produce good children; good cities made livable places for good citizens.

Concomitant with a shift in social discourse—away from the looser term "public" (as in "the" public)—architecture embraced the more prevalent term "community" to refer not to society-at-large but to a more specific and unified struggle against the powers that be. In architecture, the term is thus associated with a reaction against "top-down," "master," or even "heroic" architectures in favor of more local and rather democratic design approaches intended to solve specific problems. "Community" in architecture is considered, then, as a type of obscure client whose presence assures the redress of social ills simply through a proximity to the experience of those ills. However, as benevolent as this presence seems, the dialog with this "client" has largely resulted in the installation of decorative paving, ornamental planters, and pocket parks. As Richard Sennett noted in 1970, "community is a deceptive social term." Oddly, the invocation of this "deceptive term" signals an architecture that is (still) caught in a postmodernist bind—somehow attempting to be both locally philanthropic and universal, both institutionally embedded and reactive. Indeed, architecture is behind the times. Theorists such as Chantal Mouffe and Jürgen Habermas have long decried the term for its ambivalence and subjugation to the often-capricious flows of identity politics. Even social and political discourse, the term's supposed origin, recognizes it as largely bankrupt.

If the term is all but dead, then, to even those who make a living studying such groups and struggles, it may well be that the term's survival in architecture is only due to the object lesson it offers in precritical nostalgia. As an index of social betterment, the use of the term signals an imagined time in the discipline when architecture could use its technologies to heal the world, without asking "What technologies?" "Whose world?" and "Who's/whose healing"? Similarly, the use of the term may also signal a desire for a design process that could ironically be heroic without the burden of mastery or complete authorship, such as those urban schemes currently explored through diagramming or through the insertion of homogeneous "carpets" within a field of difference. The term may very well induce shudders, but its invocation ultimately begs post-mortem questions essential to further contemporary understandings of architecture, such as technology's hinge to betterment, the constitution of architecture's "public," and the recurrent theme of architecture's responsibility.

27. Dana Cuff

One apt characterization of the state of the contemporary in architecture is our seeming inability to comprehend or represent the present coupled with a fetishistic attention to the "near future." Perhaps the uncertainty characteristic of postmodern attention to "the now" produces a magnetic attraction to theory focused on "the next," and hence our obsession with fashion, emergent technologies, shifting notions of "cool." Even the social in architecture has followed this path, departing from the social sciences into pop culture, and literary criticism, from Venturi to Jameson. At the intersection of architecture and society forty years ago, empirical observations rendered truths (consider the research of environmental psychologists or studies of vernacular building), and these truths were surely good, and sometimes remarkably beautiful (recall the Dogon Village photographs). In the face of empiricism's undoing and the end of "culture" as a homogenizing superstructure, architectural theory prudently retreated from society.

But surely architecture is unwilling to retreat from the social entirely. Most current discourse in architecture is limited in its ability to consider politics, for example, in spite of the substantial implications political events hold for our field. If new theory is to find relevance and inform contemporary human circumstance, it will operate not within the boundaries of scientific observation, but within practices. Parallel to what Kurt Lewin, a founder of the field of social psychology, devised as "action research," research directed toward solving social problems, we might develop an "action theory" trained at sociospatial questions. This action theory would necessarily be undertaken by architectural scholars and practitioners alike.

Sociologist Anthony Giddens characterizes the counter-weight to security and trust in contemporary life as a heightened experience of risk and danger. Architectural theory that purports no connections to creating and the cultural implications of those actions is a risk-free enterprise. This was catalyzed for me when I read Cynthia Davidson's summary of the AnyBody conference in Buenos Aires, in 1995. There, the ANY group's theoretical premise of "undecidability" was challenged by Argentinians acutely aware of the need for decidedly political, social action. Davidson lobbied instead, and somewhat apologetically, to retain undecidability, which she contrasted with polarizing, dialectical ideologies, and the "separation of high and low [that] produces an unnecessary antagonism in which theory and its models are unproductively positioned against need and its demands." By so doing, she not only distances thought from action within our discipline, but she effectively constructs theory as "high" and need as "low." Thus, she avoids the dangers inherent to "steering the juggernaut," as Giddens describes our attempts to act in accordance with desired social change. While we acknowledge the end of utopian progressivism, to be left with undecidability is to be set adrift.

This brute fashioning transparently reveals the problem of re-engaging the social—further complicated by the tendency for social activism to swamp (often via moralizing or whining) all matters aesthetic, formal, and even technological. Instead, two operations can bring a new social aspect into contemporary architecture and its discourses. First, I want to argue for the decidedly speculative in architecture. Based on presumptive rather than predictive logics, it is a conjectural architecture, in Karl Popper's sense of the term, considering rather than solving problems. Second, to develop that decidedly speculative architecture requires a new attention to spatial practices. Just as ethnographers have realized that culture is written by anthropological practices rather than the resulting reports of collected facts, architects can see spatial practices not as tracings on a map but as a dynamic, poetic protocol. This can be conceived as a form of program that is broader than function, encompasses multiple subjects, engages politics and culture, and can itself be compelling and even beautiful—

The decidedly speculative formulates an action theory that stands against architecture as autonomous discourse, rejecting both a subjectivist position and a formalist stance that separate subject and object with blinding Cartesian logic. Instead, action and practices serve as the matrix for a collusion of form and humanity, space and time. The decidedly speculative is risky: it is inherently political, and at the same time, prone to failure. Repositioning the cultural in architecture in terms of practices means that we abandon the quest for truths. Instead, our task is to make something, literally, out of our social and cultural knowledge, just as we make something of our technical knowledge or our aesthetic sensibilities.

By spatial practices, I refer to situated social practices, those of the subject, the occupant/user, the consumer, the client, the architect, the culture. This is a pragmatist argument for spatial practices as inspiration, rather than as direct application or explicit instruction. We don't need to know about the spatial practices that inspired a work in order to appreciate or even understand the work. The pragmatist philosopher Richard Rorty argues for the imaginative as necessary and separate from history (the making of past ideas coherent with one another) and from natural science (the discovery of ways of describing the world which make it more predictable and manageable). Thus history and science stand in contrast to art and politics, the function of which is not known in advance and which changes our purposes. Art and politics, necessary to the architectural imaginative, require a speculative posture. Architectural speculation fundamentally reverses the opening characterization of present uncertainties that produce theories about emergent futures. A decidedly speculative architecture works in the midst of Giddens's contemporary dangers, drawing inspiration from patterns of "the now," theorizing present spatial practices in order to construct "the next." This is theory for action, defining any dialectical ideology of high and low in pragmatist terms: What can we make of it? What we make is speculative architecture, of course.

CREDITS

First published in the United States of America in 2005 by
The Monacelli Press, Inc.
611 Broadway, New York, New York 10012.

Library of Congress Cataloging-in-Publication Data
Crib sheets : notes on the contemporary architectural
conversation / edited by Sylvia Lavin and Helene Furján
with Penelope Dean.
p. cm.
Includes bibliographical references.
ISBN 1-58093-158-8
1. Architecture—Miscellanea. 2. Contemporary, The.
I. Lavin, Sylvia. II. Furján, Helene Mary, date. III. Dean,
Penelope.
NA2540.C75 2005
724'.7—dc22   2005018765

Printed and bound in China

Editors: Sylvia Lavin, Helene Furján
Associate Editor: Penelope Dean
Managing Editor: Caroline Blackburn
Design: Stephen Kinder Design Partnership

Thanks to: Ellie Abrons, Ruth Alvarez, Hyejin Cho, Russell
Fortmeyer, Yvette Garcia, Don Leeper, Beth Rosenblum,
Marc Sanchez, Ari Seligmann, Keith VanDerSys, Jon Yoder,
Jeremy Leman, Monica Ly; "The Good, the Bad, and the
Beautiful" participants, Ben van Berkel, Caroline Bos,
Preston Scott Cohen, Dana Cuff, Neil Denari, Mark Lee,
Greg Lynn, Mark Mack, Thom Mayne, Robert Somol, and
Alejandro Zaera-Polo; Christopher Waterman, Dean,
School of the Arts and Architecture, UCLA, and Pat Baxter,
Associate Dean of Administration, School of the Arts and
Architecture, UCLA.

UCLA DEPARTMENT OF ARCHITECTURE AND URBAN DESIGN
FACULTY AND VISITING CRITICS, 2000-2005

Sylvia Lavin, Chair*
Hadley Soutter Arnold
Peter Arnold, Faculty
Ann Bergren
Ben van Berkel, S. Charles Lee Chair, 2002*
Aaron Betsky, Harvey S. Perloff Chair, 2002
Johan Bettum
Petra Blaisse, Harvey S. Perloff Chair, 2004
Caroline Bos, S. Charles Lee Chair, 2002*
Bernard Cache
Preston Scott Cohen, Harvey S. Perloff Chair, 2002*
John Cordic
Dana Cuff*
Kevin Daly
Neil Denari*
Julie Eizenberg
David Erdman
Diane Favro
Eva Forgacs
Michelle Fornabai
Helene Furján
Robert Garlipp
Chris Genik
Bruce Gibbons
Joseph Giovannini
Marcelyn Gow
Zaha Hadid, Harvey S. Perloff Chair, 1998
Thomas S. Hines
Craig Hodgetts
Randolph Jefferson
Charles Jencks
Sharon Johnston
Victor Jones
Wes Jones
Ulrika Karlsson
Jeffrey Kipnis, Harvey S. Perloff Chair, 2002
Amy Kulper
Jurg Lang
Clover Lee
Mark Lee*
Robin Liggett
Alan Locke
Greg Lynn*
Mark Mack*
Marta Malé
Thom Mayne*
Rose Mendez
Murray Miline

Farshid Moussavi, S. Charles Lee Chair, 2001
Glenn Murcutt, S. Charles Lee Chair, 2000
Tim Murphy
Barton Myers
Enrique Norten, Harvey S. Perloff Chair, 2003
Martin Paull
Jason Payne
Barton Phelps
Wolf Prix, S. Charles Lee Chair, 1999
George Rand
Hani Rashid, Harvey S. Perloff Chair, 2003
Ben Refuerzo
Dagmar Richter
Heather Roberge
Michele Saee
Richard Schoen
Roger Sherman
Robert E. Somol*
Randolph Stout
Carlos Tejeda
Kostas Terzidis
Bernard Tschumi, Harvey S. Perloff Chair, 2000
Billie Tsien, Harvey S. Perloff Chair, 2001
Anthony Vidler
Richard Weinstein
Buzz Yudel
Alejandro Zaera-Polo, S. Charles Lee Visiting Professor, 2001*
Andrew Zago

*Conference participant, "The Good, the Bad, and the Beautiful," May 13, 2002

CREDITS

MATTER: Panelite LLC, Panelite Cast Polymer Series translucent honeycomb panel, 2002.

TECHNIQUE: Tord Boontje, Garland Light, 2002. Copyright Tord Boontje Studio.

PRACTICE: Gehry Partners, Le Clos Jordanne, design process model, 1999.

DIAGRAM: FOA, Yokohama International Port Terminal, structural geometry, Yokohama, Japan, 1999.

EXTREME FORM: Verner Panton, Shell Lamp ceiling, Panton's home, Basel-Binningen, 1984-85.

LANDSCAPE: Field Operations and Diller Scofidio + Renfro with Olafur Eliasson, Piet Oudolf, and Buro Happold, Friends of the High Line Design Competition, 2004. Courtesy Friends of the High Line and City of New York.

ENVIRONMENT: Julius Shulman, Kaufmann House by Richard Neutra, Palm Springs, 1947. Copyright Julius Shulman.

SURFACE: Polly Apfelbaum, *Single Gun Theory*, 2001. Synthetic crushed velvet and dye, approximately 30 x 7 ½ feet. Courtesy of the artist and D'Amelio Terras, New York. Copyright Polly Apfelbaum.

ATMOSPHERE: Olafur Eliasson, *The Weather Project*, 2004. Installation: Turbine Hall, Tate Modern, London. Courtesy Tanya Bonakdar Gallery, New York. Photo: Jens Ziehe.

DECORATION: Tom Meinhold, Madonna Inn, Barrel of Fun Suite, 2002.

STYLE: Lisa Eisner, 1959 Column Dress by Pierre Cardin, in his home on the French Rivera.

AUTONOMY: Greg Lynn FORM, Coffee and Tea Piazza 2000, Alessi, 2003.

FLOW: Char Davies, forest stream, digital frame captured in real-time through HMD (head-mounted display) during live performance of *Immersive Environment Ephemere*, 1998.

THE GENERIC: Steven Holl, Simmons Hall, MIT, Cambridge, Massachusetts, 2002. Photo: Andy Ryan.

URBANITY: Gregory Crewdson, *Untitled*, laser direct C-print, 1999. Courtesy of the artist and Luhring Augustine, New York.

GEOMETRY: Preston Scott Cohen, Tel Aviv Museum of Art, 2003. Computer rendering: Chris Hoxie.

PROGRAM: MVRDV, Les Halles, design competition, Paris, 2004.

TECHNOLOGY: Jennifer Steinkamp, *Loom*, 2003. Courtesy Acme, Los Angeles.

IMAGE: ChanSchatz, PTG.06 schivaratanond→ejoo, 2003. Acrylic and ink on canvas, 40 x 70 inches. Courtesy of the artists and Massimo Audiello, New York.

OPERATION: OMA in collaboration with John Baldessari, Caltrans District 7 Headquarters competition, 2001, Los Angeles.

CRITICALITY: Charles Jencks, Critical Modernism Evolutionary Tree, 2000.

COMMUNITY: Alex S. MacLean and Landslides, Opposing cul-de-sacs, built/not built, Houston, Texas, 1999.

MATTER

1. Sanford Kwinter, "Beat Science," lecture, Berlage Institute, May 2004.
2. Sheila Kennedy, "Electrical Effects: (A) Material Media," *Praxis* 6 (2004): 84.
3. Ellen Lupton, "SKIN: New Design Organics," in *Skin: Surface, Substance, and Design* (New York: Princeton Architectural Press, 2002), 30.
4. Gilles Deleuze, *Francis Bacon: The Logic of Sensation*, trans. Daniel Smith (Minneapolis: University of Minnesota Press, 2002), 86.
6. William Gibson, *Virtual Light* (New York: Bantam Books, 1994), 70.
7. Jesse Reiser, "Solid State Architecture," in *Reiser + Umemoto: Recent Projects*, ed. Andrew Benjamin (London: Academy Editions, 1998), 50.
9. Hugh Ferriss, *The Metropolis of Tomorrow* (1929; New York: Princeton Architectural Press, 1986), 124.
10. Mark Goulthorpe, "Precise Indeterminacy," interview, *Praxis* 6 (2004): 37.
11. Manuel De Landa, "Deleuze, Diagrams, and the Genesis of Form," *ANY* 23 (1998): 30.
12. Jeffrey Kipnis, "On the Wild Side" (1999), in Foreign Office Architects, *Phylogenesis: foa's Ark* (Barcelona: Actar, 2003), 572.
13. Gilles Deleuze and Félix Guattari, *A Thousand Plateaus: Capitalism and Schizophrenia*, trans. Brian Massumi (Minneapolis: University of Minnesota Press, 1987), 141.
16. Bruce Sterling, "Literary Freeware: Not For Commercial Use," lecture, Rice Design Alliance, March 2, 1994.

TECHNIQUE

2. Mark Goulthorpe, "Precise Indeterminacy," interview, *Praxis* 6 (2004): 30.
3. Ben van Berkel and Peter Trümmer, "Between Ideogram and Image-Diagram," *OASE* 48 (1998): 71.
4. Achim Menges, "Morpho-Ecologies: Approaching Complex Environments," *Architectural Design Profile* 169 (2004): 83.
5. Frank Gehry, *Gehry Talks: Architecture + Process*, ed. Mildred Friedman (New York: Universe, 2002), 48.
7. François Burkhardt, "Design and 'Avant-Postmodernism,'" in *Design After Modernism: Beyond the Object*, ed. John Thackara (New York: Thames and Hudson, 1988), 147.
8. Peter Eisenman, "miMISes READING: does not mean A THING," in *Mies Reconsidered*, ed. John Zukowsky (New York: Rizzoli, 1986), 96.
9. MVRDV, *Metacity Datatown* (Rotterdam: 010 Publishers, 1999), 18.

10. Otto Wagner, *Modern Architecture*, trans. Harry Francis Mallgrave (Los Angeles: Getty Center, 1988), 86.
11. Sanford Kwinter, "Hydraulic Vision," in *Mood River* (exhibition catalog, Columbus: Wexner Center for the Arts, 2002), 33.
12. Michael Hensel, "Finding Exotic Form: An Evolution of Form Finding as a Design Method," *Architectural Design Profile* 169 (2004): 29.
13. Alejandro Zaera-Polo, "Roller-Coaster Construction," *Architectural Design: Contemporary Processes in Architecture*, Vol. 1, No. 71 (2002): 85.
15. John Thackara, ed., *Design After Modernism: Beyond the Object* (New York: Thames and Hudson, 1988), 11.
16. Rem Koolhaas, *S, M, L, XL* (New York: The Monacelli Press, 1995), 1225.
17. Sulan Kolatan and William MacDonald, "Lumping," *Architectural Design: Contemporary Processes in Architecture*, Vol. 1, No. 71 (2002): 79.
21. Jean Baudrillard, "Design and Environment," *For a Critique of the Political Economy of the Sign*, trans. Charles Levin (St. Louis: Telos Press, 1981), 186.
22. Ali Rahim, "Potential Performative Effects," *Architectural Design: Contemporary Processes in Architecture*, Vol. 1, No. 71 (2002): 55-58.

PRACTICE

1. Bernard Tschumi, *Event-Cities* (Cambridge, Mass.: MIT Press, 1994), 11.
2. MVRDV, "Excursions on Density," *El Croquis* 111: *MVRDV 1997-2002* (2002): 10.
3. Mark Wigley, "Whatever Happened to Total Design?" *Harvard Design Magazine*, Summer 1998, 21.
4. Emergence and Design Group (Michael Hensel, Michael Weinstock, Achim Menges), "Emergence in Architecture," *Architectural Design Profile* 169 (2004): 6.
5. Cecil Balmond in conversation with Michael Weinstock, "The Digital and the Material," *Architectural Design: Contemporary Processes in Architecture*, Vol. 1, No. 71 (2002): 47.
6. Steven Johnson, *Emergence: The Connected Lives of Ants, Brains, Cities, and Software* (New York: Touchstone, 2001), 177.
7. Michael Sorkin, "Frozen Light," in *Gehry Talks: Architecture + Process*, ed. Mildred Friedman (New York: Universe, 2002), 32.
8. Frank Gehry, *Gehry Talks: Architecture + Process*, ed. Mildred Friedman (New York: Universe, 2002), 52.
9. Sylvia Lavin, "Plasticity at Work," in *Mood River* (exhibition catalog, Columbus: Wexner Center for the Arts, 2002), 74.

CREDITS

11. Jonathan Hill, *The Illegal Architect* (London: Black Dog, 1998), 26.

13. Stan Allen, "From Object to Field," *Architectural Design*, Vol. 67, No. 5-6 (May-June 1997): 24.

14. Polly Apfelbaum, "Conversation with Polly Apfelbaum," *Art Journal* 63, No. 2 (Summer 2004): 84.

15. Paul Virilio, "The Overexposed City," *Zone 1/2*, republished in *Architecture Theory Since 1968*, ed. K. Michael Hays (Cambridge, Mass.: MIT Press, 1998), 544.

16. Bruce Mau, "Styling Life," in *Life Style Bruce Mau*, (London: Phaidon, 2000).

17. Bernard Tschumi, "Illustrated Index: Themes from the Manhattan Transcripts," *AA Files* 4 (1983): 67.

18. Mark Cousins, "Building an Architect," in *Occupying Architecture: Between the Architect and the User*, ed. Jonathan Hill (London/New York: Routledge, 1998), 16.

19. Servo, "Interactive Opportunities," *Architectural Design: Contemporary Processes in Architecture*, Vol. 1, No. 71 (2002): 18.

20. Frederick Kiesler, "Magical Architecture," in *Programs and Manifestoes on Twentieth-Century Architecture*, ed. Ulrich Conrads, trans. Michael Bullock (Cambridge, Mass.: MIT Press, 1964), 150.

21. Alejandro Zaera-Polo and Farshid Moussavi (FOA), "Code Remix 2000," *2G* 16 (2000): 122.

24. Walter Gropius, "Programme of the Staatliches Bauhaus in Weimar," in *Programs and Manifestoes on Twentieth-Century Architecture*, ed. Ulrich Conrads, trans. Michael Bullock (Cambridge, Mass.: MIT Press, 1964), 50.

25. Sanford Kwinter, "The Gay Science [What is Life?]," in *Life Style Bruce Mau* (London: Phaidon, 2000), 36.

26. Mark Goulthorpe, "Precise Indeterminacy," interview, *Praxis* 6 (2004): 35.

DIAGRAM

1. Gilles Deleuze, *Foucault*, trans. Séan Hand (Minneapolis: University of Minnesota Press, 1988), 34.

2. Ben van Berkel and Peter Trümmer, "Between Ideogram and Image-Diagram," *OASE* 48 (1998): 65.

3. Pia Ednie-Brown, "The Texture of Diagrams: Reasonings on Greg Lynn and Francis Bacon," *Daidalos* 74 (2000): 72.

4. Le Corbusier, *The Modulor I and II* (Cambridge, Mass.: Harvard University Press, 1982), 61.

5. MVRDV, *Metacity Datatown* (Rotterdam: 010 Publishers, 1999), 18.

6. Cecil Balmond, *Informal* (Munich: Prestel, 2002), 222-23.

7. Toyo Ito, "Diagram Architecture," *El Croquis* 77 (1996): 18.

8. Manuel De Landa, "Deleuze, Diagrams, and the Genesis of Form," *ANY* 23 (1998): 34.

9. Jeffrey Kipnis, "On Those Who Step into the Same River . . .," in *Mood River* (exhibition catalog, Columbus: Wexner Center for the Arts, 2002), 40.

10. Albert Pope, *Ladders* (Houston/New York: Rice University School of Architecture/Princeton Architectural Press, 1996), 19.

11. Stan Allen, "Diagrams Matter," *ANY* 23 (1998): 18.

12. Rem Koolhaas, *Content: Triumph of Realization*, eds. Rem Koolhaas and Brendan McGetrick (Cologne: Taschen, 2004), 20.

13. Michael Sorkin, "See You in Disneyland," in *Variations on a Theme Park* (New York: Hill and Wang, 1992), 214-15.

14. Andrew Benjamin, "Lines of Work: On Diagrams and Drawing," *Architectural Philosophy* (London: Athlone, 2000), 154-55.

15. Margaret Crawford, "The World in a Shopping Mall," in *Variations on a Theme Park*, ed. Michael Sorkin (New York: Hill and Wang, 1992), 7.

16. R. E. Somol, "In the Wake of Assemblage," *Assemblage* 41 (2000): 93.

17. Jesse Reiser, "Solid State Architecture," in *Reiser + Umemoto: Recent Projects*, ed. Andrew Benjamin (London: Academy Editions, 1998), 51.

18. Sanford Kwinter, "Landscapes of Change: Boccioni's *Stati d'animo* as a General Theory of Models," *Assemblage* 19 (1992): 63.

19. Gilles Deleuze and Félix Guattari, *A Thousand Plateaus: Capitalism and Schizophrenia*, trans. Brian Massumi (Minneapolis: University of Minnesota Press, 1987), 141-42.

EXTREME FORM

2. Jeffrey Kipnis, "Towards a New Architecture," *Architectural Design Profile* 102 (1993): 42.

3. Sanford Kwinter, "Landscapes of Change: Boccioni's *Stati d'animo* as a General Theory of Models," *Assemblage* 19 (1992): 58.

4. Greg Lynn, "Blobs, or Why Tectonics Is Square and Topology Is Groovy," *ANY* 14 (1996): 58.

5. Hugh Ferriss, *The Metropolis of Tomorrow* (1929; New York: Princeton Architectural Press, 1986), 60.

6. René Thom, *Structural Stability and Morphogenesis: An Outline of a General Theory of Models* (Massachusetts: Addison-Wesley, 1972), 13.

7. Ellen Lupton, "SKIN: New Design Organics," in *Skin: Surface, Substance, and Design* (New York: Princeton Architectural Press, 2002), 34.

8. Lars Lerup, *After the City* (Cambridge, Mass.: MIT Press, 2000), 51.

10. Michael Hensel, "Finding Exotic Form: An Evolution of Form Finding as a Design Method," *Architectural Design Profile* 169 (2004): 27.

12. Neil Leach, "Swarm Tectonics: A Manifesto for an Emergent Architecture," *Archis* 5 (2002): 39.

14. Manuel De Landa, "Deleuze and the Use of the Genetic Algorithm in Architecture," *Architectural Design: Contemporary Techniques in Architecture*, Vol. 72, No. 1 (2002): 11.

15. Cecil Balmond, *Informal* (Munich: Prestel, 2002), 14.

16. Sylvia Lavin, "Plasticity at Work," in *Mood River* (exhibition catalog, Columbus: Wexner Center for the Arts, 2002), 80.

18. Gilles Deleuze and Félix Guattari, *A Thousand Plateaus: Capitalism and Schizophrenia*, trans. Brian Massumi (Minneapolis: University of Minnesota Press, 1987), 497-98.

LANDSCAPE

1. Reyner Banham, "The Great Gizmo," in *A Critic Writes* (Berkeley/Los Angeles: University of California Press, 1996), 110.

2. Charlotte E. Mauk, ed., *Yosemite and the Sierra Nevada: Photographs by Ansel Adams, Selections from the Works of John Muir* (Boston: Houghton Mifflin Company, 1948), 38.

4. Gordon Cullen, *Townscape* (London: Architectural Press, 1961), 10.

5. J. B. Jackson, *Discovering the Vernacular Landscape* (New Haven: Yale University Press, 1984), 3.

6. Rem Koolhaas, Bruce Mau, Petra Blaisse, et al., "Tree City," in *CASE: Downsview Park Toronto*, ed. Julia Czerniak (Munich: Prestel, 2001), 80.

7. Robert Venturi, Denise Scott Brown, Steven Izenour, *Learning from Las Vegas* (Cambridge, Mass.: MIT Press, 1972), 10.

8. Michael Sorkin, "See You in Disneyland," in *Variations on a Theme Park* (New York: Hill and Wang, 1992), 210.

9. Michael Hensel, "Ocean North-Surface Ecologies," in *Landscape Urbanism: A Manual for the Machinic Landscape*, eds. Mohsen Mostafavi and Ciro Najle (London: AA Publications, 2003), 111.

10. Sanford Kwinter, "Landscapes of Change: Boccioni's *Stati d'animo* as a General Theory of Models," *Assemblage* 19 (1992): 63.

11. Andrew Ross, *The Celebration Chronicles* (New York: Ballantine Publishing, 1999), 88.

12. Jean Baudrillard, *America*, trans. Chris Turner (London: Verso, 1988), 127.

13. Paul Goldberger, "Orange County: Tomorrowland—Wall to Wall," *New York Times*, December 11, 1988, 32.

14. Roberto Burle Marx, *Christian Science Monitor*, August 1986, 25.

15. Alex Wall, "Programming the Urban Surface," in *Recovering Landscape: Essays in Contemporary Landscape Architecture*, ed. James Corner (New York: Princeton Architectural Press, 1999), 233.

16. Cecil Balmond in conversation with Michael Weinstock, "The Digital and the Material," *Architectural Design: Contemporary Processes in Architecture*, Vol. 1, No. 71 (2002): 48-49.

17. *Emergency State: First Responder and Law Enforcement Training Architecture*, exhibition, Center for Land Use Interpretation, Los Angeles (May-August 2004).

18. Keller Easterling, "Error," in *Landscape Urbanism: A Manual for the Machinic Landscape*, eds. Mohsen Mostafavi and Ciro Najle (London: AA Publications, 2003), 154.

19. Detlef Mertins, "landscapeurbanismhappensintime," in *Landscape Urbanism: A Manual for the Machinic Landscape*, eds. Mohsen Mostafavi and Ciro Najle (London: AA Publications, 2003), 136.

20. Mohsen Mostafavi, "Landscapes of Urbanism," in *Landscape Urbanism: A Manual for the Machinic Landscape*, eds. Mohsen Mostafavi and Ciro Najle (London: AA Publications, 2003), 7.

21. Alejandro Zaera-Polo and Farshid Moussavi (FOA), "Code Remix 2000," *2G* 16 (2000): 124.

22. Robert Smithson, "The Spiral Jetty," in *Robert Smithson: The Collected Writings*, ed. Jack Flam (Berkeley/Los Angeles: University of California Press, 1996), 146.

23. Reyner Banham, *Los Angeles: The Architecture of Four Ecologies* (London: Penguin, 1971), 235.

ENVIRONMENT

2. Lars Lerup, *After the City* (Cambridge, Mass.: MIT Press, 2000), 52.

3. Siegfried Kracauer, *The Mass Ornament*, trans. Thomas Y. Levin (Cambridge, Mass.: Harvard University Press, 1995), 183.

5. Mark Wigley, "The Architecture of Atmosphere," *Daidalos* 68 (1998): 24.

6. Michael Sorkin, "See You in Disneyland," in *Variations on a Theme Park* (New York: Hill and Wang, 1992), 207.

7. Robert Venturi, Denise Scott Brown, Steven Izenour, *Learning from Las Vegas* (Cambridge, Mass.: MIT Press, 1972), 49.

8. Peter Blake, *God's Own Junkyard: The Planned Deterioration of America's Landscape* (New York: Holt, Rinehart and Winston, 1964), 8.

9. Sylvia Lavin, "Richard Neutra and the Psychology of the American Spectator," *Grey Room* 1 (Fall 2000): 44.

10. Mark Goulthorpe, "Precise Indeterminacy," interview, *Praxis* 6 (2004): 33.

11. Greg Lynn, "A New Style of Life," in *Latent Utopias: Experiments within Contemporary Architecture*, eds. Zaha Hadid and Patrick Schumacher (exhibition catalog, Graz: Steirischer, 2002), 146.

12. Philip Johnson, 1975 address at Columbia University, in *Simpson's Contemporary Quotations*, comp. James B. Simpson (Boston: Houghton Mifflin, 1988), 247-48.

13. Achim Menges, "Morpho-Ecologies: Approaching Complex Environments," *Architectural Design Profile* 169 (2004): 81.

14. Richard Neutra, *Survival Through Design* (New York: Oxford University Press, 1954), 138.

CREDITS

15. Reyner Banham, *Los Angeles: The Architecture of Four Ecologies* (London: Penguin, 1971), 240.

16. Michael Hensel, "Finding Exotic Form: An Evolution of Form Finding as a Design Method," *Architectural Design Profile* 169 (2004): 29.

17. Paul Virilio, "The Overexposed City," in *Architecture Theory Since 1968*, ed. K. Michael Hays (Cambridge, Mass.: MIT Press, 1998), 543.

18. Reyner Banham, *The Architecture of the Well-Tempered Environment* (Chicago: University of Chicago Press, 1969), 129.

21. Brett Steele, "Ambient and Augmented," in *Latent Utopias: Experiments within Contemporary Architecture*, eds. Zaha Hadid and Patrick Schumacher (exhibition catalog, Graz: Steirischer, 2002), 95.

23. Rem Koolhaas, "Junkspace," in *Content: Triumph of Realization*, eds. Rem Koolhaas and Brendan McGetrick (Cologne: Taschen, 2004), 162.

25. Constant, "New Babylon: Outline of a Culture," in *Constant's New Babylon: The Hyper-Architecture of Desire*, ed. Mark Wigley (Rotterdam: 010 Publishers, 1998), 160.

27. Jean Baudrillard, *America*, trans. Chris Turner (London: Verso, 1988), 127.

28. Stephen Bayley, *Sex, Drink and Fast Cars* (New York: Pantheon Books, 1987), 77.

29. Marc Augé, *Non-Places: Introduction to an Anthropology of Supermodernity*, trans. John Howe (London/New York: Verso, 1995), 79.

SURFACE

1. As cited in Nancy Jo Troy, *The De Stijl Environment* (Cambridge, Mass.: MIT Press, 1983), 139.

2. Sheila Kennedy, "Electrical Effects: (A) Material Media," *Praxis* 6 (2004): 89.

3. Sylvia Lavin, "The Temporary Contemporary," *Perspecta* 34 (2003): 134-35.

4. Alex Wall, "Programming the Urban Surface," in *Recovering Landscape: Essays in Contemporary Landscape Architecture*, ed. James Corner (New York: Princeton Architectural Press, 1999), 233.

5. Frei Otto, in conversation with Emergence and Design Group, *Architectural Design Profile* 169 (2004): 20.

6. Emergence and Design Group (Michael Hensel, Michael Weinstock, Achim Menges), "Fit Fabric: Versatility Through Redundancy and Differentiation," *Architectural Design Profile* 169 (2004): 41.

8. Guy Julier, *The Culture of Design* (London: SAGE Publications, 2002), 149.

9. Ellen Lupton, "SKIN: New Design Organics," in *Skin: Surface, Substance, and Design* (New York: Princeton Architectural Press, 2002), 30-31.

11. Gottfried Semper, *Style* (Los Angeles: Getty, 2004), 438-39.

12. Michael Hensel, "Ocean North-Surface Ecologies," in *Landscape Urbanism: A Manual for the Machinic Landscape*, eds. Mohsen Mostafavi and Ciro Najle (London: AA Publications, 2003), 111.

13. Cecil Balmond in conversation with Michael Weinstock, "The Digital and the Material," *Architectural Design: Contemporary Processes in Architecture*, Vol. 1, No. 71 (2002): 47.

14. Paul Virilio, "The Overexposed City," in *Zone 1/2*, eds. Jonathan Crary et al. (Baltimore: Johns Hopkins University Press, 1985), 17-21.

ATMOSPHERE

2. Olafur Eliasson, "Seeing Yourself Sensing," in *Olafur Eliasson*, eds. Madeleine Grynsztejn, Daniel Birnbaum, and Michael Speaks (London: Phaidon, 2002), 127.

3. Lars Lerup, *After the City* (Cambridge, Mass.: MIT Press, 2000), 46.

4. William Gibson, *Virtual Light* (New York: Bantam Books, 1994), 109.

5. Jeffrey Kipnis, "On Those Who Step into the Same River . . . ," in *Mood River* (exhibition catalog, Columbus: Wexner Center for the Arts, 2002), 40.

6. Rachel Carson, *Silent Spring* (New York: Fawcett Crest, 1962), 5.

7. Gilles Deleuze, *Francis Bacon: The Logic of Sensation*, trans. Daniel Smith (Minneapolis: University of Minnesota Press, 2002), 31.

9. Sebastian Weber and Kai Vöckler, "Luminous Bodies," *Daidalos* 68 (1998): 28.

10. Mark Wigley, "The Architecture of Atmosphere," *Daidalos* 68 (1998): 18.

11. Alison and Peter Smithson, "Letter to America" in *Ordinariness and Light* (Cambridge, Mass.: MIT Press, 1970), 141.

12. Dave Hickey, *Air Guitar* (Los Angeles: Art Issues Press, 1997), 52.

13. Richard Neutra, *Survival Through Design* (New York: Oxford University Press, 1954), 145.

14. Andy Warhol, *The Philosophy of Andy Warhol (From A to B and Back Again)* (San Diego/New York/London: Harvest, 1975), 159.

15. John Ruskin, "The Opening of the Crystal Palace Considered in Some of Its Relations to the Prospects of Art," in *The Works of John Ruskin* 12 (London: Longmans, 1904), 419.

19. Constant, "New Babylon: Outline of a Culture," in *Constant's New Babylon: The Hyper-Architecture of Desire*, ed. Mark Wigley (Rotterdam: 010 Publishers, 1998), 165.

20. Jean Baudrillard, *The System of Objects*, trans. James Benedict (London/New York: Verso, 1996), 30.

21. Gernot Böhme, "Atmosphere as an Aesthetic Concept," *Daidalos* 68 (1998): 112-14.

25. Ben van Berkel and Caroline Bos, *Effects: Radiant Synthetic, Move* 3 (Amsterdam: UN Studio/Goose, 1992), 141.

DECORATION

1. Robert Venturi, *Complexity and Contradiction in Architecture* (New York: Museum of Modern Art, 1966), 25.

2. As quoted in Matei Calinescu, *Five Faces of Modernity* (Durham: Duke University Press, 1987), 251.

3. Jeffrey Kipnis, "The Cunning of Cosmetics," *El Croquis* 84 (1997): 25.

4. Frank Gehry, *Gehry Talks: Architecture + Process*, ed. Mildred Friedman (New York: Universe, 2002), 266.

5. Rem Koolhaas, "Junkspace," in *Content: Triumph of Realization*, eds. Rem Koolhaas and Brendan McGetrick (Cologne: Taschen, 2004), 163.

6. Jennifer Bloomer, ". . . and *venustas*," *AA Files* 25 (Summer 1993): 3.

7. Jean Baudrillard, *The System of Objects*, trans. James Benedict (London/New York: Verso, 1996), 26.

8. Clement Greenberg, *Art and Culture: Critical Essays* (Boston: Beacon, 1961), 10.

9. Mark Wigley, *White Walls, Designer Dresses: The Fashioning of Modern Architecture* (Cambridge, Mass.: MIT Press, 1995), 7.

10. www.madonnainn.com.

12. Adolf Loos, "Ornament and Education," in *Ornament and Crime: Selected Essays*, ed. Adolf Opel (Riverside, Calif.: Ariadne, 1998), 187.

13. Walter Benjamin, *The Arcades Project*, trans. Howard Eiland and Kevin McLaughlin (Cambridge, Mass./London: Belknap Press, 1999), 213.

15. Sylvia Lavin, "The Temporary Contemporary," *Perspecta* 34 (2003): 130.

23. As quoted in Matei Calinescu, *Five Faces of Modernity* (Durham: Duke University Press, 1987), 250.

STYLE

1. Naomi Klein, *No Logo* (London: Flamingo, 2001), 73.

2. "Conversation with Polly Apfelbaum," *Art Journal* 63, No. 2 (Summer 2004): 85.

4. Ben van Berkel and Caroline Bos, *Effects: Radiant Synthetic, Move* 3 (Amsterdam: UN Studio/Goose Press, 1999), 27.

5. Alejandro Zaera-Polo and Farshid Moussavi (FOA), "Code Remix 2000," *2G* 16 (2000): 126.

6. R. E. Somol, "Twelve Reasons to Get Back into Shape," in *Content: Triumph of Realization*, eds. Rem Koolhaas and Brendan McGetrick (Cologne: Taschen, 2004), 86-87.

7. Andy Warhol, *The Philosophy of Andy Warhol (From A to B and Back Again)* (San Diego/New York/London: Harvest, 1975), 77.

8. Bruce Mau, *Life Style Bruce Mau* (London: Phaidon, 2000), 27.

9. Robert Venturi, Denise Scott Brown, Steven Izenour, *Learning from Las Vegas* (Cambridge, Mass.: MIT Press, 1972), 48.

10. Reyner Banham, *A Critic Writes* (Berkeley/Los Angeles: University of California Press, 1997), 6.

11. Hugh Ferriss, *The Metropolis of Tomorrow* (1929; New York: Princeton Architectural Press, 1986), 30.

12. Jürgen Habermas, "Modernity: An Incomplete Project," in *The Anti-Aesthetic: Essays on Postmodern Culture*, ed. Hal Foster (Port Townsend, Wash.: Bay Press, 1983), 4.

13. Sanford Kwinter, "The Gay Science [What is Life?]," in *Life Style Bruce Mau* (London: Phaidon, 2000), 35.

14. James Traub, "Trumpologies," *New York Times Magazine*, September 12, 2004, 36.

15. William Gibson, *Pattern Recognition* (New York: G. P. Putnam's Sons, 2003), 2.

17. Michael Speaks, "Individualization Without Identity," in *City Branding: Image Building & Building Images*, eds. Urban Affairs and Véronique Patteeuw (Rotterdam: NAI, 2002), 60.

18. Hans Ibelings, *Supermodernism: Architecture in the Age of Globalization* (Rotterdam: NAI, 2002), 135.

19. Rem Koolhaas, *Delirious New York: A Retroactive Manifesto for Manhattan* (1978; New York: The Monacelli Press, 1994), 148-50.

21. As quoted in Matei Calinescu, *Five Faces of Modernity* (Durham: Duke University Press, 1987), 251.

22. Bruce Sterling, "When Blobjects Rule the Earth," lecture, *SIGGRAPH*, August 2004.

23. Charles Jencks, *Architecture 2000: Predictions and Methods* (New York: Praeger Publishers, 1971), 91.

AUTONOMY

1. *The Deerhunter* (1978), screenplay by Michael Cimino and Deric Washburn.

2. Hans Hollein, "Alles ist Architektur," in *Architecture Culture 1943-1968: A Documentary Anthology*, ed. Joan Ockman (New York: Columbia Books of Architecture/ Rizzoli, 1993), 460-62.

5. Reyner Banham, *Los Angeles: The Architecture of Four Ecologies* (London: Penguin, 1971), 23.

6. Bernard Rudofsky, *Behind the Picture Window* (New York: Oxford University Press, 1955), 177.

7. Dave Hickey, *Air Guitar* (Los Angeles: Art Issues Press, 1997), 9.

8. Jeffrey Kipnis, "In the Mood for Architecture," *Anything*, ed. Cynthia C. Davidson (Cambridge, Mass./New York: MIT Press/Anyone, 2001), 96.

11. Brian Massumi, *Parables for the Virtual: Movement, Affect, Sensation* (Durham: Duke University Press, 2002), 35.

15. K. Michael Hays, "Prolegomenon for a Study Linking the Advanced Architecture of the Present to that of the 1970s through Ideologies of Media, the Experience of Cities in Transition, and the Ongoing Effects of Reification," *Perspecta* 32 (2000): 101.

18. Peter Eisenman, "Autonomy and the Will to the Critical," *Assemblage* 41 (2000): 91.

21. R. E. Somol, "In the Wake of Assemblage," *Assemblage* 41 (2000): 93.

FLOW

1. Toyo Ito in conversation with Cecil Balmond, "Concerning Fluid Spaces," *A+U* 404 (2004): 45.

2. Le Corbusier, *The Modulor I and II* (Cambridge, Mass.: Harvard University Press, 1982), 107.

3. Mark C. Taylor, *The Moment of Complexity: Emerging Network Culture* (Chicago/London: University of Chicago Press, 2001), 3.

4. Rem Koolhaas, "Junkspace," in *Content: Triumph of Realization*, eds. Rem Koolhaas and Brendan McGetrick (Cologne: Taschen, 2004), 162.

5. Srdjan Jovanovic Weiss and Sze Tsung Leong, "Escalator," in *Project on the City 2: Harvard Design School Guide to Shopping*, eds. Rem Koolhaas et al. (Cologne: Taschen, 2001), 337.

6. Saskia Sassen, *Cities in a World Economy* (Thousand Oaks, Calif.: Pine Forge Press, 1994), 2.

8. John Thackara, "Perceiving Flow," *Archis* 5 (2002): 14.

9. Sanford Kwinter, "Hydraulic Vision," in *Mood River* (exhibition catalog, Columbus: Wexner Center for the Arts, 2002), 32.

10. Fredric Jameson, *Postmodernism, or the Cultural Logic of Late Capitalism* (Durham: Duke University Press, 1991), 43.

11. Manuel Castells, *The Rise of the Network Society*, Vol. 1, *The Information Age: Economy, Society and Culture* (Malden, Mass./Oxford: Blackwell, 2000), 442.

12. Jeffrey Kipnis, "On Those Who Step into the Same River . . . ," in *Mood River* (exhibition catalog, Columbus: Wexner Center for the Arts, 2002), 36.

13. Alex Wall, "Programming the Urban Surface," in *Recovering Landscape: Essays in Contemporary Landscape Architecture*, ed. James Corner (New York: Princeton Architectural Press, 1999), 234.

14. Ole Bouman, "Total Mobilmachung," *Archis* 5 (2002): 4.

15. Steven Johnson, *Emergence: The Connected Lives of Ants, Brains, Cities, and Software* (New York: Touchstone, 2001), 232.

16. Stan Allen, *Points + Lines: Diagrams and Projects for the City* (New York: Princeton Architectural Press, 1999), 101.

17. Luciana Parisi and Tiziana Terranova, "Heat-Death: Emergence and Control in Genetic Engineering and Artificial Life," *CTheory* 84 (www.ctheory.net, posted 5/10/2000): 1.

THE GENERIC

1. As quoted in Virginia Postrel, *The Substance of Style* (New York: HarperCollins, 2003), 19-20.

4. Marc Augé, *Non-Places: Introduction to an Anthropology of Supermodernity*, trans. John Howe (London/New York: Verso, 1995), 111.

5. Manuel Castells, *The Rise of the Network Society*, Vol. 1, *The Information Age: Economy, Society and Culture* (Malden, Mass./Oxford: Blackwell, 2000), 429-30.

7. Hans Ibelings, *Supermodernism: Architecture in the Age of Globalization* (Rotterdam: NAI, 2003), 65-66.

8. Hal Foster, *Design and Crime* (London/New York: Verso, 2002), 17.

9. Michael Speaks, "Individualization Without Identity," in *City Branding: Image Building & Building Images*, eds. Urban Affairs and Véronique Patteeuw (Rotterdam: NAI, 2002), 54.

10. Rem Koolhaas, "The Generic City," *S, M, L, XL* (New York: The Monacelli Press, 1995), 1249-50.

12. Guy Debord, *The Society of the Spectacle*, trans. Donald Nicholson-Smith (New York: Zone Books, 1994), 123.

16. Steven Miles, *Consumerism as a Way of Life* (London: SAGE Publications, 1998), 36-42.

URBANITY

1. Ed W. Soja, "Inside Exopolis: Scenes from Orange County," in *Variations on a Theme Park*, ed. Michael Sorkin (New York: Hill and Wang, 1992), 95.

2. Peter Blake, *God's Own Junkyard: The Planned Deterioration of America's Landscape* (New York: Holt, Rinehart and Winston, 1964), 17.

3. Manuel Castells, *The Rise of the Network Society*, Vol. 1, *The Information Age: Economy, Society and Culture* (Malden, Mass./Oxford: Blackwell, 2000), 417.

4. Lars Lerup, *After the City* (Cambridge, Mass.: MIT Press, 2000), 47.

5. Frank Lloyd Wright, as quoted in *Simpson's Contemporary Quotations*, comp. James B. Simpson (Boston: Houghton Mifflin, 1988), 249.

6. Dolores Hayden, *A Field Guide to Sprawl* (New York/London: Norton, 2004).

7. Le Corbusier, as quoted in *Simpson's Contemporary Quotations*, comp. James B. Simpson (Boston: Houghton Mifflin, 1988), 248.

8. Steven Flusty, "Building Paranoia," in *Architecture of Fear*, ed. Nan Ellin (New York: Princeton Architectural Press, 1997), 57.

9. MVRDV, *Metacity Datatown* (Rotterdam: 010 Publishers, 1999), 16.

11. Robert Venturi, Denise Scott Brown, Steven Izenour, *Learning from Las Vegas* (Cambridge, Mass.: MIT Press, 1972), 11.

12. Gilles Deleuze and Félix Guattari, *A Thousand Plateaus: Capitalism and Schizophrenia*, trans. Brian Massumi (Minneapolis: University of Minnesota Press, 1987), 500.

13. Marc Augé, *Non-Places: Introduction to an Anthropology of Supermodernity*, trans. John Howe (London/New York: Verso, 1995), 109.

14. J. G. Ballard, "Project for a Glossary of the Twentieth Century," in *Zone 6: Incorporations*, eds. Jonathan Crary and Sanford Kwinter (New York: Urzone, 1992), 273.

15. Michael Weinstock, "Morphogenesis and the Mathematics of Emergence," *Architectural Design Profile* 169 (2004): 11.

16. Albert Pope, *Ladders* (Houston/New York: Rice University School of Architecture/Princeton Architectural Press, 1996), 3.

19. Mike Davis, *City of Quartz: Excavating the Future in Los Angeles* (New York: Vintage Books, 1992), 4.

22. Reyner Banham, *Los Angeles: The Architecture of Four Ecologies* (London: Penguin, 1971), 213.

24. Kevin Lynch, *The Image of the City* (Cambridge, Mass.: MIT Press, 1960), 2.

GEOMETRY

1. Sanford Kwinter, "Landscapes of Change: Boccioni's *Stati d'animo* as a General Theory of Models," *Assemblage* 19 (1992): 58.

2. Jesse Reiser, "Solid State Architecture," in *Reiser + Umemoto: Recent Projects*, ed. Andrew Benjamin (London: Academy Editions, 1998), 51.

6. Greg Lynn, "Blobs, or Why Tectonics Is Square and Topology Is Groovy," *ANY* 14 (1996): 58.

7. Mark C. Taylor, *The Moment of Complexity: Emerging Network Culture* (Chicago/London: University of Chicago Press, 2001), 183.

8. Ben van Berkel and Peter Trümmer, "Between Ideogram and Image-Diagram," *OASE* 48 (1998): 64-65.

9. Cecil Balmond, *Informal* (Munich: Prestel, 2002), 226-27.

10. Gilles Deleuze and Félix Guattari, *A Thousand Plateaus: Capitalism and Schizophrenia*, trans. Brian Massumi (Minneapolis: University of Minnesota Press, 1987), 499.

11. Jeffrey Kipnis, "Towards a New Architecture," *Architectural Design Profile* 102 (1993): 47.

13. OCEAN North (Michael Hensel, Kivi Sotama), "Vigorous Environments," *Architectural Design: Contemporary Techniques in Architecture*, Vol. 72, No. 1 (2002): 41.

18. Michael Weinstock, "Morphogenesis and the Mathematics of Emergence," *Architectural Design Profile* 169 (2004): 11.

PROGRAM

2. Richard Neutra, *Survival Through Design* (New York: Oxford University Press, 1954), 111.

4. Peter Eisenman, "Post-Functionalism," *Architecture Theory Since 1968*, ed. K. Michael Hays (Cambridge, Mass.: MIT Press, 1998), 239.

5. Jesse Reiser, "Loose Fit," in *Reiser + Umemoto: Recent Projects*, ed. Andrew Benjamin (London: Academy Editions, 1998), 32.

6. William Gibson, *Virtual Light* (New York: Bantam Books, 1994), 70.

7. Ben van Berkel and Peter Trümmer, "Between Ideogram and Image-Diagram," *OASE* 48 (1998): 65.

8. Robert Venturi, Denise Scott Brown, Steven Izenour, *Learning from Las Vegas* (Cambridge, Mass.: MIT Press, 1972), 44.

9. Raymond M. Hood, "A City under a Single Roof," in Manfredo Tafuri, *The Sphere and the Labyrinth: Avant-Gardes and Architecture from Piranesi to the 1970s*, trans. Pellegrino d'Acierno and Robert Connolly (Cambridge, Mass.: MIT Press, 1987), 193.

10. Rem Koolhaas, *Delirious New York: A Retroactive Manifesto for Manhattan* (1978; New York: The Monacelli Press, 1994), 197.

11. Greg Lynn, "Blobs, or Why Tectonics Is Square and Topology Is Groovy," *ANY* 14 (1996): 61.

12. MVRDV, *FARMAX* (Rotterdam: 010 Publishers, 1998), 396.

15. Sylvia Lavin, "Plasticity at Work," in *Mood River* (exhibition catalog, Columbus: Wexner Center for the Arts, 2002), 74.

TECHNOLOGY

1. Reyner Banham, *The Architecture of the Well-Tempered Environment* (Chicago: University of Chicago Press, 1984), 312.

2. Jesse Reiser and Nanako Umemoto, "West Side Convergence: Urban Processes," *Architectural Design: Contemporary Processes in Architecture*, Vol. 70, No. 3 (2000): 87.

3. Paul Virilio, "The Overexposed City," in *Zone 1/2*, eds. Jonathan Crary et al. (Baltimore: Johns Hopkins University Press, 1985), 18.

4. Chris Wise, "Drunk in an Orgy of Technology," *Architectural Design Profile* 169 (2004): 57.

5. Mark Goulthorpe, "Precise Indeterminacy," interview, *Praxis* 6 (2004): 30.

6. Richard Neutra, *Survival Through Design* (New York: Oxford University Press, 1954), 101.

7. Buckminster Fuller, as quoted in *Simpson's Contemporary Quotations*, comp. James B. Simpson (Boston: Houghton Mifflin, 1988), 247.

8. Steven Johnson, *Emergence: The Connected Lives of Ants, Brains, Cities, and Software* (New York: Touchstone, 2001), 208.

9. Ellen Lupton, "SKIN: New Design Organics," in *Skin: Surface, Substance, and Design* (New York: Princeton Architectural Press, 2002), 30.

10. Guy Julier, *The Culture of Design* (London: SAGE Publications, 2002), 35.

CREDITS

11. OCEAN North (Michael Hensel, Kivi Sotama), "Vigorous Environments," *Architectural Design: Contemporary Techniques in Architecture*, Vol. 72, No. 1 (2002): 40.

12. Anthony Vidler, *The Architectural Uncanny: Essays in the Modern Unhomely* (Cambridge, Mass.: MIT Press, 1992), 148.

14. Adrian Franklin, "Consuming Design, Consuming Retro," in *The Changing Consumer: Markets and Meanings*, eds. Steven Miles, Alison Anderson, and Kevin Meethan (London: Routledge, 2002), 91-92.

17. Dawn Finley and Mark Wamble, "Notes on System Form: The Rest of the World Exists," *Perspecta* 34 (2003): 110.

19. Frank Gehry, *Gehry Talks: Architecture + Process*, ed. Mildred Friedman (New York: Universe, 2002), 52.

20. Michael Hensel, "Finding Exotic Form: An Evolution of Form Finding as a Design Method," *Architectural Design Profile* 169 (2004): 31.

22. Sanford Kwinter, "Architecture and the Technologies of Life," *AA Files* 27 (Summer 1994): 3.

IMAGE

1. Alison and Peter Smithson, "But Today We Collect Ads," in *The Independent Group: Postwar Britain and the Aesthetics of Plenty*, ed. David Robbins (Cambridge, Mass.: MIT Press, 1991), 185.

2. Peter Eisenman, in conversation with Alejandro Zaera-Polo at the Berlage Institute, Rotterdam, October 7, 2002.

3. Ryue Nishizawa, "Seeing the Sendai Mediatheque," in *Case: Toyo Ito, Sendai Mediatheque*, eds. Ron Witte and Hiroto Kobayashi (Munich: Prestel, 2002), 26.

4. Barry Katz, "The Arts of War: 'Visual Presentation' and National Intelligence," *Design Issues* 12, No. 2 (1996): 7.

5. Walter Benjamin, *Illuminations*, trans. Harry Zohn (New York: Schocken, 1968), 239.

6. Sergei M. Eisenstein, "Montage and Architecture," *Assemblage* 10 (1989): 128.

7. K. Michael Hays, "Abstraction's Appearance (Seagram Building)," in *Autonomy and Ideology*, ed. R. E. Somol (New York: The Monacelli Press, 1997), 283-85.

8. Charles Jencks, *Architecture 2000* (New York/Washington: Praeger Publishers, 1971), 93.

9. Bernard Tschumi, "Illustrated Index: Themes from the Manhattan Transcripts," *AA Files* 4 (1983): 69.

10. Kevin Lynch, *The Image of the City* (Cambridge, Mass.: MIT Press, 1960), 9.

11. Deyan Sudjic, *Cult Objects* (London: Paladin Granada, 1985), 113.

12. Hubert Damisch, *Skyline: The Narcissistic City*, trans. John Goodman (Stanford: Stanford University Press, 2001), 12.

13. Robert Venturi, Denise Scott Brown, Steven Izenour, *Learning from Las Vegas* (Cambridge, Mass.: MIT Press, 1972), 4.

14. Paul Virilio, "The Overexposed City," in *Architecture Theory Since 1968*, ed. K. Michael Hays (Cambridge, Mass.: MIT Press, 1998), 550.

15. Michael Sorkin, "Frozen Light," in *Gehry Talks: Architecture + Process*, ed. Mildred Friedman (New York: Universe, 2002), 32.

16. Jean Baudrillard, *Simulations* (New York: Semiotext(e), 1983), 11.

17. Gilles Deleuze and Félix Guattari, *A Thousand Plateaus: Capitalism and Schizophrenia*, trans. Brian Massumi (Minneapolis: University of Minnesota Press, 1987), 494.

18. Jesse Reiser, "Solid State Architecture," in *Reiser + Umemoto: Recent Projects*, ed. Andrew Benjamin (London: Academy Editions, 1998), 49.

19. Bernard Rudofsky, *Behind the Picture Window* (New York: Oxford University Press, 1955), 195.

20. Herbert J. Gans, *The Levittowners: Ways of Life and Politics in a New Suburban Community* (New York: Pantheon Books, 1967), 282.

21. Beatriz Colomina, "Enclosed by Images: The Eameses' Multimedia Architecture," *Grey Room* 2 (Winter 2001): 7.

25. Sylvia Lavin, "Inter-Objective Criticism: Bernard Tschumi and Le Fresnoy," *ANY* 21 (1997): 34-35.

OPERATION

2. Hashim Sarkis, *CASE: Le Corbusier's Venice Hospital and the Mat Building Revival* (Munich: Prestel, 2001), 13.

3. Richard Neutra, *Survival Through Design* (New York: Oxford University Press, 1954), 43.

4. Rem Koolhaas, interview with Sarah Whiting, *Assemblage* 40 (1999): 47.

5. Sheila Kennedy, "Electrical Effects: (A) Material Media," *Praxis* 6 (2004): 89.

6. MVRDV, *Metacity Datatown* (Rotterdam: 010 Publishers, 1999), 18.

8. Michael Speaks, "Individualization Without Identity," in *City Branding: Image Building & Building Images*, eds. Urban Affairs and Véronique Patteeuw (Rotterdam: NAI 2002), 60.

9. Michel de Certeau, *The Practice of Everyday Life*, trans. Steven Rendall (Berkeley/Los Angeles: University of California Press, 1984), xv.

10. Michel Foucault, "Of Other Spaces: Utopias and Heterotopias," in *Architecture Culture 1943-1968: A Documentary Anthology*, ed. Joan Ockman (New York: Columbia Books of Architecture/Rizzoli, 1993), 420.

11. Charles Jencks, *Architecture 2000: Predictions and Methods* (New York: Praeger Publishers, 1971), 91.

12. Stan Allen and James Corner, "Lifescape: Field Operations," *Praxis* 4 (2002): 24.

14. Alex Wall, "Programming the Urban Surface," in *Recovering Landscape: Essays in Contemporary Landscape Architecture*, ed. James Corner (New York: Princeton Architectural Press, 1999), 234.

15. Sanford Kwinter, "Landscapes of Change: Boccioni's *Stati d'animo* as a General Theory of Models," *Assemblage* 19 (1992): 60-61.

16. Bruce Mau, *Life Style Bruce Mau* (New York: Phaidon, 2000), 238.

19. Michael Weinstock, "Morphogenesis and the Mathematics of Emergence," *Architectural Design Profile* 169 (2004): 11.

20. Sylvia Lavin, "Inter-Objective Criticism: Bernard Tschumi and Le Fresnoy," *ANY* 21 (1997): 32.

22. Mark Goulthorpe, "Precise Indeterminacy," interview, *Praxis* 6 (2004): 43.

26. Manuel de Landa, "Deleuze and the Use of the Genetic Algorithm in Architecture" (2001), in Foreign Office Architects, *Phylogenesis: foa's Ark* (Barcelona: Actar, 2003), 521, 529.

28. Steven Johnson, *Emergence: The Connected Lives of Ants, Brains, Cities, and Software* (New York: Touchstone, 2001), 163.

CRITICALITY

2. Antonio Gramsci, *Prison Notebooks*, trans. Quintin Hoare and Geoffrey Nowell Smith (New York: International Publishers, 1971), 173.

3. Peter Eisenman, "Autonomy and the Will to the Critical," *Assemblage* 41 (2000): 91.

5. Michael Speaks, "Alternatives to Resistance," *Praxis* 5 (2003): 19.

6. Herbert Muschamp, "How the Critic Sees," *ANY* 21 (1997): 16.

7. Jean Baudrillard, "The Ecstasy of Communication," in *The Anti-Aesthetic: Essays on Postmodern Culture*, ed. Hal Foster (Port Townsend, Wash.: Bay Press, 1983), 130.

9. Gregory Ulmer, *Heuretics: The Logic of Invention* (Baltimore: John Hopkins University Press, 1994), 14.

10. Marshall McLuhan, *Understanding Media: The Extensions of Man* (1964; Cambridge, Mass.: MIT Press, 1994), 26.

12. Sanford Kwinter, "There Is No Such Thing as 'Post-Critical,' Only Good and Bad Design," *Praxis* 5 (2003): 21.

13. Peter Eisenman, "Post-Critical Architecture," *Casabella* 644 (1999): 1.

14. Maurice Nadeau, *The History of Surrealism* (New York: Macmillan Company, 1965), 240.

19. Manfredo Tafuri, *Theories and Histories of Architecture* (London: Granada, 1980), 153.

20. K. Michael Hays, "After Critique, Whither?" *Praxis* 5 (2003): 16.

23. Jeffrey Kipnis, "On the Wild Side" (1999), in Foreign Office Architects, *Phylogenesis: foa's Ark* (Barcelona: Actar, 2003), 569.

COMMUNITY

1. As cited in Dolores Hayden, *A Field Guide to Sprawl* (New York/London: Norton, 2004), glossary.

3. Charles Baudelaire, as cited in John Bartlett, *Bartlett's Familiar Quotations* (Boston: Little, Brown, and Company, 2002), 525.

4. Edward J. Blakely and Mary Gail Snyder, "Divided We Fall: Gated and Walled Communities in the United States," in *Architecture of Fear*, ed. Nan Ellin (New York: Princeton Architectural Press, 1997), 85.

6. Tom Wolfe, *From Bauhaus to Our House* (New York: Farrar, Straus & Giroux, 1981), 21.

8. As quoted in "Heir to the White Shoes," *Sydney Morning Herald: Good Weekend*, November 16, 2002.

9. Marc Augé, *Non-Places: Introduction to an Anthropology of Supermodernity*, trans. John Howe (London/New York: Verso, 1995), 103, 111-12.

10. Mark Landesbaum and Heidi Evans, "Mission Viejo: Winning Is the Only Game in Town," *Los Angeles Times*, August 22, 1984.

12. Rem Koolhaas, *Delirious New York: A Retroactive Manifesto for Manhattan* (1978; New York: The Monacelli Press, 1994), 152.

13. Bernard Rudofksy, *Behind the Picture Window* (New York: Oxford University Press, 1955), 195.

14. Marshall Berman, *All That Is Solid Melts into Air: The Experience of Modernity* (Middlesex: Penguin, 1988), 291.

15. Mike Davis, *City of Quartz: Excavating the Future in Los Angeles* (London: Pimlico, 1998), 223.

16. Doorn Manifesto (Jacob Bakema, Aldo van Eyck, H. P. Daniel van Ginkel, Hans Hovens-Greve, Peter Smithson, John Voelker), "CIAM Meeting 29-30, January 31, 1954," in *Architecture Culture 1943-1968: A Documentary Anthology*, ed. Joan Ockman (New York: Columbia Books of Architecture/Rizzoli, 1993), 183.

17. J. G. Ballard, *Cocaine Nights* (London: Flamingo, 1996), 219.

19. Lynn Spigel, "The Suburban Home Companion: Television and the Neighborhood Ideal in Postwar America," in *Sexuality and Space*, ed. Beatriz Colomina (New York: Princeton Architectural Press, 1992), 186.

20. Michael Speaks, "Individualization Without Identity," in *City Branding: Image Building & Building Images*, eds. Urban Affairs and Véronique Patteeuw (Rotterdam: NAI, 2002), 58.

CREDITS

... author of over twenty books for children and young ... in Northamptonshire with her husband and three cats.

Acclaim for Set in Stone:

'I found myself bathing in the wonderful descriptions . . .
Newbery writes with grace and immediacy'
Daily Telegraph

'This novel calls to mind the writings of the Brontë sisters . . . despite
or maybe because of the author seeming so unconcerned with current
trends, this book works on every level. The plot is full of twists, the
charcters are multi-dimensional, and the atmosphere of that grand
Victorian house, with all its intrigue and hierarchy, is electric. *Set in
Stone* is a gripping page-turner for children and adults alike'
Glasgow Herald

'An absorbing, thoughtful, jigsaw puzzle of a book . . . if its
atmosphere is that of a Victorian mystery, the setting combines the
richly imagined detail of a George Eliot novel with the grace and
light of a Vuillard painting'
Kate Agnew, Books for Keeps

'Linda Newberry has very successfully recreated the nineteenth
century voice reminiscent of the Bronte's and Austen, and the
element of mystery to be solved evokes the style of Wilkie Collins.
The particular strength of this novel is the way in which the
characters are drawn, each with their own story that leads the
reader through the quagmire that is the Farrow family saga . . .
most suited to older teenagers and adults'
Writeaway!

'A gothic romance dealing with the most taboo subject of all . . .
Newbery has created a climactic period story, compelling in its
description and psychological drama . . . the relationship between
art and life is starkly framed'
TES

'Masterpiece of storytelling'
Oxford Times

'The protagonists' unreliable narratives keep readers on the edge
of their seats as the shocking nature of their secret is gradually,
teasingly revealed in this lyrical novel'
The Bookseller

Also by Linda Newbery:

THE SHELL HOUSE

SISTERLAND